Making S...
Englis...
Money M...

English in Use Series
General Editor: David Crystal

Other titles in the series:
Making Sense of English Usage
Making Sense of Foreign Words in English

Making Sense of
English in
Money Matters

Ean Taylor

Chambers

Published 1991 by W & R Chambers Ltd
43–45 Annandale Street, Edinburgh EH7 4AZ

A catalogue record for this book is available from the
British Library

ISBN 0-550-18039-7

Printed in England by Clays Ltd, St Ives plc

Contents

Foreword

Like millions of others, over the years I have had bank accounts, mortgages and insurance policies. Like millions of others, I have attempted to understand the language of the documents relating to my bank accounts, mortgages and insurance policies. Sometimes I have succeeded. More usually, I have failed, and have had to ask the advice of friends who work in banks, building societies and insurance offices. Sometimes this has helped. More usually, it hasn't, for these friends speak to me in the language of their profession, made worse by the fact that the spoken medium does not allow me the opportunity to read and reread and reread. . . .

I have often prayed for a book which would help me to make some progress in understanding what everyone is talking about, and how they talk about it. Ean Taylor's book has given me the stick I need. I have already found it helpful and practical in its explanations of what goes on behind the counters and across the desks of the main high-street institutions which look for and after our money. *Money Matters* is a cross between an encyclopedic introduction to the world of personal finance and a lexicographical check-list of the meaning and history of the words belonging to this world. Whether you treat it as encyclopedia or dictionary, the result will be the same—growing illumination and confidence, and a gradually dawning awareness that the language used by the people behind those desks and counters isn't as impenetrable a barrier as you thought it was. Whether it will save you any money is a moot point. Whether it will make you any money is a moot point. But at least you'll be more aware of what's going on, as you count and consider, and that can be no bad thing.

David Crystal

Preface

Two, probably overlapping, sets of terms form the subject matter of this dictionary. The first set comprises those words and phrases which the staffs of the High Street institutions use to their customers, but which are often less than fully comprehended by the latter (eg *answer, cancel, quota*). The main purpose of presenting such terms as these is to promote better understanding between the providers and the recipients of the financial services which these institutions make available.

The second group of terms comprises those which may be overheard by customers but which are essentially 'backstage language' (eg *cross-firing, hit rate, reference list*). Despite the efforts of their marketing departments and advertising agencies over the last few decades, the High Street institutions can still be forbidding ones for many people, and I hope that the varying degrees of linguistic informality, humour and innovation demonstrated in the coining of such terms as these will help to show a more human side of the staff concerned.

A brief explanation of the boundaries imposed on the dictionary may be useful. It would have been tempting to produce a book which embraced all British financial institutions: the Bank of England, the commercial banks, the Stock Exchange, investment and unit trusts, the commodities and futures markets, and many other, more esoteric, organizations. Such a work, though, would have run the risk of losing its integrity. To retain coherence, therefore, the present dictionary restricts itself to the major bodies which vie with one another in the High Street for the surplus funds of the general public—the banks, the building societies, and the life assurance companies.

One of the perennial difficulties in working in the field of language varieties is that of deciding at what point the specialized merges with the general. If one explains a term which turns out to be widely understood, one's efforts are redundant; conversely, one may choose not to include a particular item, only to discover that clarification would have been welcomed. The decision will always be subjective, and one can only hope to strike a fair balance.

It is hoped, then, that anyone who has, or is contemplating having, dealings with the institutions covered by this book will find the explanations offered to be of value. The head office and branch staffs of the institutions themselves will also probably have a natural interest in a description and discussion of their specialized language. Not least, academics of various kinds, and linguists in particular, may be attracted to what is presented here. The latter have long been able to study language which varies geographically and/or socially, but the present work is one of very few available on 'occupational dialects'. The appendices which deal with etymological and functional matters may warrant special attention by these readers.

Making acknowledgments should be one of the most pleasant and straightforward parts of an undertaking such as this. In fact, finding a satisfactory method of recording my debt to all those who furthered the work turns out to be almost impossible. So many people assisted in so many ways that to name them all would take several pages. Furthermore, as many respondents provided information at more than one stage of the research, to specify contributions would result in much repetition of details. To this must be added the facts that the names of staff who completed questionnaires were never known to me, and that some other contributors specifically requested anonymity. So, to the parent organizations involved (some 50 in number) and to the individuals concerned (several hundred), this acknowledgment has to operate as a blanket but nonetheless sincere expression of thanks.

Fortunately, some others can receive a less impersonal mention. Professor John Widdowson of the University of Sheffield supervised the original thesis from which some of the terms discussed are taken, whilst David Crystal's editorial comments have been constantly helpful, and I am grateful to them both. To David Taylor must go much of the credit for this work ever being word-processed at all. Describing himself as a 'technological tooth fairy', he would come in the night to remedy all the author's attempts to wreck both the hardware and the software during the day. His ability is matched only by his tenacity.

It is customary at this point to add a comment to the effect that, notwithstanding all the advice and support received, blemishes must remain, and that these are the fault of no one but the author. Whilst this is largely true in the present case too, I must end with a rider. All living languages are in a state of change, and few more so than the one described in the following pages. So, if you read them as a 'practitioner' and find yourself saying, 'We don't use the term X anymore, but Y', or if you are a customer baffled by a financial neologism, please write and let me know. I really will be pleased to hear from you.

Pronunciation Guide

Vowels

i:	need	/ni:d/
ɪ	pit	/pɪt/
i	very	/'vɛri/
ɛ	pet	/pɛt/
æ	pat	/pæt/
ʌ	other	/'ʌðəʳ/
ʊ	book	/bʊk/
u:	too	/tu:/
u	influence	/'ɪnfluəns/
ɒ	cough	/kɒf/
ɔ:	ought	/ɔ:t/
ɜ:	work	/wɜ:k/
ə	another	/ən'ʌðəʳ/
ɑ:	part	/pɑ:t/

Glides

eɪ	plate	/pleɪt/
aɪ	sigh	/saɪ/
ɔɪ	ploy	/plɔɪ/
oʊ	go	/goʊ/
aʊ	now	/naʊ/
ɪə	hear	/hɪəʳ/
ɛə	fair	/fɛəʳ/
ʊə	poor	/pʊəʳ/

Consonants

p	pit	/pɪt/
b	bit	/bɪt/
t	ten	/tɛn/
d	den	/dɛn/
k	cap	/kæp/
g	gap	/gæp/
ʃ	shin	/ʃɪn/
ʒ	pleasure	/'plɛʒəʳ/
ʧ	chin	/ʧɪn/
ʤ	budge	/bʌʤ/
h	hit	/hɪt/
f	fit	/fɪt/
v	very	/'vɛri/
θ	thin	/θɪn/
ð	then	/ðɛn/
s	sin	/sɪn/
z	zones	/zoʊnz/
m	meat	/mi:t/
n	knit	/nɪt/
ŋ	sing	/sɪŋ/
l	line	/laɪn/
r	rid	/rɪd/
j	yet	/jɛt/
w	quick	/kwɪk/

ʳ indicates an 'r' pronounced only before a following vowel
' precedes the syllable with primary stress

Guide to Readers

Bold type, eg **shot coin** at **bagged coin**, **meet** at **banker's drafts** or **turn** under **base rate**, is used to refer the reader to other entries in the book.

A

accountant

In banking, a now obsolescent name for the person responsible for the general day-to-day administration of a bank branch, ie with immediate responsibility for those who deal with transactions on the accounts. The person is not, as the name is almost certain to suggest to the uninitiated, a member of one of the accounting bodies, such as a Chartered Accountant. In one bank, the accountant's full title is *Branch Accountant, General Office*, which may sound like a gift to those who enjoy puffed-up designations. In practice, however, this bit of titular grandiloquence is normally punctured by the substitution of a deflating acronym: requests for decisions on administrative matters made to those not competent to adjudicate may be deflected with the words, 'I'm sorry, you'll have to refer that to the BAGO /'bægoʊ/ '.

Just as much of the work on customers' accounts is now handled in regional or centralized computing offices, so the term *accountant* is fast disappearing, being replaced by titles such as *Administration Manager* and *Operations Manager*.

account payee

See **crossing**

activate slip

In banking and building societies, a small piece of paper, sent out to a customer in connection with a plastic card, which has to be returned to the issuing branch before the card can be used.

actuary

In life assurance, someone with a mathematical or statistical background who is employed by an **assurance** or **insurance** company to calculate risks, bearing in mind the likelihood of certain eventualities. An actuary's professional body is the Institute of Actuaries. Actuaries' skills are much valued in assessing, for example, the size of a **lump sum** in relation to the probable number of years that an **annuity** would be payable to a customer of a given age. They have been known to tell the self-deprecatory joke that their profession is suited to those who would find the life of a chartered accountant too exciting.

added rate
See **turn**

additional voluntary contributions
In banking, building societies and life assurance, a fairly self-explanatory term: employees who are members of a company pension scheme can choose to augment their pension when they retire by opting to pay larger contributions to the scheme during their working life.

See also **free standing additional voluntary contributions**

advance
In banking, building societies and life assurance, a loan by another name. Holden's *Securities for Bankers' Advances* was required reading for candidates for the Associateship examinations during the author's banking days. Institutions make it function as a verb, too: 'We are prepared to advance you the sum of £x.'

advise
In banking, building societies and life assurance, to tell. *Advise* has long been preferred in commercial contexts requesting or providing information. Despite cajolings and injunctions in the house manuals provided for the guidance of staff, the longer, Latinate word continues to hold sway over the shorter Anglo-Saxon *tell*: 'We are advising you that your account is overdrawn to the extent of . . .'; 'I shall be pleased if you will advise me of the date of the transaction'.

AFBD
See **Association of Futures Brokers and Dealers**

agent

In banking, building societies and life assurance, someone who acts on behalf of a particular company. Many estate agents act as agents for building societies, effectively running limited services from their premises alongside their normal work. In a different but related field, agents or **representatives** of a named company in investments business (life **assurance** and pensions, for example) have no obligation to recommend policies or other **products** from any company other than the one for whom they act, and thus contrast with **independent financial advisers.**

See also **best advice**

allocation

See **quota 1**

annual percentage rate (of charge)

In banking, building societies and life assurance, a quotation intended to give would-be borrowers a standard measure of the actual cost of credit; normally abbreviated to **APR**. As indicated under **flat rate**, it is hardly ever the case that a loan is repaid in one fell swoop; generally, principal and interest are repaid, say, monthly. Thus, if you borrow £100 at a flat rate of 10 per cent on 1 January for a period of one year, with repayments to be made on the first day of each month, it is only for the 31 days of January that you actually owe £100. The average sum borrowed over the whole year is in fact little more than £50. For this reason, the true rate will be just short of double the flat rate. If there are handling charges, arrangement fees, and the like, these all have to be taken into account as well in calculating the APR, which will consequently, of course, be even higher.

Those with a head for the arithmetical details of the equations used in the formulae for arriving at specific APRs should consult the booklet entitled *The True Cost of Credit*, issued by the Office of Fair Trading.

annuity

In life assurance, an arrangement whereby customers hand over **lump sums** to **assurance** companies in return for guaranteed income for the rest of their lives. Both company and customer are taking a risk (in the company's case, professionally calculated by an **actuary**) on how long this arrangement will last—the longer the better as far as the customer is concerned, of course. Cynical though it may seem to point out, the opposite is true for the company.

answer

In banking, a reason for returning a cheque unpaid, or instructions to the 'beneficiary' of an unpaid cheque, written by the **paying bank** at the top left-hand corner of such a cheque. Many of these answers may not be immediately comprehensible to the reader, who may have to raise the matter of non-payment with the **drawer**. For ease of reference, the answers most likely to cause difficulty are grouped together below.

Postdated, hardly a common word, means that the cheque bears a date later than that of the day on which it arrives at the **paying bank**. Uncertainty is also likely in the case of *Out of Date*, which refers to the fact that a cheque was presented for payment more than six months after its date.

Effects not cleared is used where a banker returns a cheque because, although the credit balance on the drawer's account appears to be sufficient to cover the cheque, the items that make up all or part of that balance have been paid in so recently that they themselves may still be returned unpaid. A particular danger in this area is what the banker refers to as *cross-firing*. This may take several forms, but the most common involves one person maintaining accounts at two different branches, on each of which is simultaneously drawn a cheque for the credit of the other. The situation will continue to be aggravated until one manager realizes what is happening, and decides to return one of the cheques marked *Effects not cleared*. A comparatively new twist has been given to this old trick by customers who maintain credit card accounts in addition to their normal current accounts. It is possible to 'repay' part of the debt to the credit card company with a cheque on the current account, which is in turn replenished by funds withdrawn in cash from the card account. This is an especially nasty one for the banks to deal with: as the banks have substantial investment in the major credit-card companies, returning cheques payable to those companies is tantamount to returning cheques payable to themselves.

Payment countermanded by order of drawer This answer must present problems to many who are confronted with it. It means that the person who signed the cheque has decided to instruct the bank not to pay it after all.

The banker's term for the tearing into pieces of a cheque is *mutilation.* If a cheque presented for payment has been torn all the way through (and that point is crucial), then the banker will take this as a *prima facie* indication that the cheque should not be paid—it could have been 'destroyed' by the drawer and then improperly reconstituted by the payee. In such cases, the banker will return the item, marked *Mutilated cheque.* If, as quite frequently happens, a cheque is accidentally torn by the payee in the act of opening the envelope that encloses it, the paying banker will require both a statement to that effect and a corroborating statement by the **collecting bank** to be endorsed on the cheque. If only the former statement appears, the cheque will still be returned, this time with the answer *Statement re mutilation requires banker's confirmation.*

In some cases, the reason for the retention of these terms lies in their precision and succinctness: *effects* neatly encompasses all the items that may be credited to an account— cheques, other bills of exchange, dividend warrants, etc— whilst *cleared* has an exact technical meaning (ie passed through the clearing house, or presented direct, and paid by the bank on which it is drawn) that is not readily expressed in a few words. In other cases, however, sheer inertia must be the explanation: it is difficult to see otherwise why the much more widely understood term *stopped* should not be substituted for *countermanded.*

On the face of it, one particular answer, *Refer to Drawer*, is perfectly innocuous—in theory, one might want to take up any number of technical matters concerning the cheque. In practice, however, the instruction has only one implication—'We're sending this back for you to sort out with the drawer, because there isn't enough money in (or agreed overdraft **limit** on) the account with us to cover it'. The reason banks use this euphemistic approach is their contractual obligation not to disclose information about their customers' affairs: to write *Insufficient funds*, for example, on a **dishonoured** cheque would clearly be in breach of that duty.

A slightly more optimistic version of this answer is *Refer to Drawer, Please Represent*, which holds out the hope that if the cheque is put through the system again there is the possibility that it will be paid.

See **present** for further discussion of this particular answer

asdate

/'æzdeɪt/ In building societies, to show an item of business in the accounting records under the date on which it should have appeared, where the actual transaction has taken place on a different date. This useful verb has been coined as a direct result of computerization. **Credits** accepted by societies may not be processed by the computer until the following working day. As a society's rules stipulate that money should earn interest from the day of receipt, the computer form listing a day's transactions may include a column headed *As date*, showing the date which will appear on a customer's statement and which will be used for the purposes of calculating interest. This adverbial phrase has been conveniently combined into the single verb *asdate*, so that if an item of business is unavoidably held over until the next day, the manager can say to a clerk, 'Put it through tomorrow and asdate it for today.'

Asdate provides a good example of the way in which neologisms may be imperceptibly assimilated into the language. The immediate reaction of informants to the suggestion that the word was a recent coinage was twofold: they protested that it was not at all new (that they had 'always known it') and that it appeared on their societies' internal forms. Only after they had checked the precise wording on the forms and reported back did they admit that the actual heading is the phrase *As date*, and that none of them, in fact, had ever encountered *asdate* in print. Their ultimate amazement (not too strong a word)—and delight—derived from learning that they were playing a significant part in the propagation of a verb whose structure is unprecedented: *asdate* appears to be the only verb in the language formed by treating the *as* of an adverbial phrase as a particle to be prefixed to a noun. The *Oxford English Dictionary* does record that 'with many common adjectives and adverbs *as . . .*was formerly written in combination, especially in idiomatic constructions, eg *asmuch, aswell . . .*', and we have the Modern English *inasmuch*, so that *asdate* may claim respectable antecedents; nevertheless, its particular form of procreation remains unique.

ASR

In building societies, the initial letters of the elliptical sentence, **all signatures required**, indicating that the holders of an account in joint names have stipulated that they must all sign for each transaction.

See also **ESTO**

assets

See **equity**

assign

In banking, building societies and life assurance, usually, to transfer the right to receive money. The three types of High Street institution whose language is the subject of this book are neatly brought together by *assign*, in that mortgagees (eg banks and building societies) look favourably on life **assurance** polices as **security** (see **mortgage**). Obviously, such security is only of any worth if the mortgagee can obtain the benefits under the policy if the mortgagor (the customer) does not repay the loan for which the policy is acting as security. It is common, therefore, for a borrower to be asked to sign a document assigning the right to the lender to collect the **proceeds** of the policy. Naturally, there is a provision built in to the effect that, once the loan has been repaid, the lender will *reassign* the policy to the customer, so that the original position is restored.

Association of Futures Brokers and Dealers (AFBD)

One of the five **self-regulating organizations** in the UK assisting the **Securities and Investment Board** in providing some measure of protection to investors, as authorized by the Secretary of State for Trade and Industry under the Financial Services Act of 1986. The *futures* here are forward commodity and financial markets, ie those which permit dealing in tea, sugar, cotton, etc or financial securities, where delivery is promised on a specified future date at a specified price.

assurance

In life assurance, cover provided against an event that is certain to happen; hence, *whole life assurance*, where a sum is payable on the death of the **life assured**, and *endowment assurance*, where a sum is payable on a specified date or on the death of the life assured, whichever is the earlier. These are available *with profits* or *without profits*, ie sharing or not in the investment fortunes of the company. Needless to say, the **premiums** on the former are higher than on the latter.

Many people working in this occupational area think it unfortunate that they have been saddled with the two words *insurance* and *assurance*. They occasionally have to explain that the essential difference between the two resides in the likelihood of the occurrence of certain events. On the one hand, you insure against the mere possibility of, say, having your car damaged or stolen. On the other hand, a person will undoubtedly either reach a particular age or die—one may be assured of that. Put another way, it is not life that is assured, but death. Needless to say, life assurance staff do not feel compelled to dwell on this point.

Perhaps for precisely that reason, it needs to be added that the distinction is far from carefully observed, with references to *life insurance* being common in both contexts. A brief glossary issued by the Association of British Insurers (which encompasses those handling assurance business) goes so far as to claim that 'the terms *insurance* and *assurance* are now interchangeable.'

See also **keyman assurance**, **term assurance**

ATM

See **automated teller machine**

audit

In building societies, widely used in its 'ordinary' sense of 'check the accuracy of accounting records'. However, it occasionally gives building-society investors undue cause for concern when it is used in letters which say, for example, 'We should be grateful if you would bring in your book so that we may audit it.' Customers who receive such a letter need not (normally) fear that they are under suspicion of 'cooking' their **passbooks**: *audit* here means nothing more than 'bring up to date', as when transactions have taken place without the passbook being presented.

audit book

In building societies, a book used to record changes of names, addresses, etc.

See also **audit**

authorized signatory

In banking, building societies and life assurance, a member of branch staff authorized by head office to sign letters and other documents issued by the branch. Many financial institutions have undergone dramatic changes during the present century: two of the greatest affecting their internal structures have been the huge increases in staff and the amalgamation of small, single-premises companies into large, multi-branch organizations. A typical feature of such concerns is that, within a branch, while several score of clerks may be employed to deal with correspondence (among other matters), the letters that they write in the course of their duties may be signed by only a few authorized signatories. Whereas a current account holder receiving a letter in the last quarter of the nineteenth century would most probably have found it to have been composed, penned and signed by the bank manager himself, the customer's 1990s counterpart would be likely to have a letter drafted by one person, typed or word-processed by another, and signed by a third.

automated (or automatic) teller machine (ATM)

In banking and building societies, machines which will issue banknotes, usually in multiples of £5 or £10, provided that the customer inserts the appropriate plastic card, correctly keys in a **personal identification number**, and of course has sufficient **funds** available; frequently referred to as *cash dispensers* by the general public, and as **ATMs** by branch staff. Increasingly, other services are on offer via an ATM, such as a display of the balance of your account or the provision of a statement by post.

The term, and the machine, are American in origin, as is indicated by the word *teller*. Although having a long history in British English, *teller* in the sense of 'money handler' is little used in the UK, where **cashier** prevails.

AVCs

See **additional voluntary contributions**

B

back
In banking, a synonym occasionally encountered for **endorse**.

BACS
See **clearing**

bagged coin
In banking, coin counted out and placed in small bags containing standard amounts, eg £5 of silver, £10 in 50p pieces. It is the opposite of **shot coin**.

balance
In banking and building societies, the difference between the total of the **credit** items on an account and the total of the **debits**—in other words, the amount left available to the customer or owing to the institution. When used as a verb, it means bringing both sides of an account to the same figure.

See also **difference**

bank charges
In banking, sums levied periodically and charged to customers' accounts as the price for handling transactions. It is now frequently possible to avoid such charges by maintaining a specified minimum credit balance on your account. Interest accrued on **loans** and **overdrafts** is usually applied at the same time, whereas other charges for special items, such as the purchase of foreign currency, are normally taken on the spot. In all these cases, payment of the costs is much less avoidable.

banker's drafts
In banking, a generic term encompassing *drafts on head office*, *drafts on branches*, and *branch cheques*. Unless a bank has received specific instructions from a customer that an

amount paid in is to be used to **meet** a certain cheque on presentation, it must not 'earmark' funds on its customer's account. It quite frequently happens that, where a large amount is involved in a transaction, the creditor is not prepared to accept a personal cheque. In such a case, the debtor may make a cheque payable to his or her own bank, which will in turn issue a **draft** on itself: this can be drawn on the bank's head office, or on another of its branches, or on its customer's own branch. In theory, and to a large extent still in practice, the point of this exercise is that, unlike the value of a customer's cheque, the value of such a draft is undisputed. Unfortunately this is decreasingly the case, as methods of forging blank banker's drafts become more sophisticated.

Although a banker's draft looks and functions like a cheque, a lawyer would maintain a distinction between the two. A cheque is a particular type of 'bill of exchange', part of the definition of which is that it must be 'addressed by one person to another' (Bills of Exchange Act, 1882, Section 3), and a banker's draft, being drawn by an institution on itself, does not satisfy this requirement.

banker's order

In banking, instructions given in writing by a customer to a bank for the latter to make regular payments from the former's account. A century ago, when access to banking services was available to only a small minority of the population, a customer might reasonably refer to *my banker*, suggesting the same sort of personal relationship that is (perhaps) still indicated in a phrase such as *in the hands of my solicitor*. With the spread of branch banking and the fairly rapid turnover of staff within the system, this personal relationship has largely disappeared; consequently, customers tend to think of their *bank* rather than their bankers. (In yet a third professional field, a parallel change may be taking place as a result of the growth of group medical practices. Casual conversation suggests that patients are now more likely to mention *a visit to the doctor's*, to consult whichever partner is available, rather than a visit to *my* [ie regular] *doctor*.)

Only bank personnel and financial commentators are now likely to use the term *bankers*. The fossilization here may be attributable to the fact that the body setting the appropriate professional examinations and representing its members enjoys the title of the *Chartered Institute of Bankers.*

The term *banker's order* is possibly now obsolescent, *standing order* being preferred by most customers and staff.

See also **direct debit**

bank rate
In banking, the old basis for calculating interest rates—the predecessor of **minimum lending rate**, itself now suspended. Individual banks now set their own **base rates**, although still under indirect influence from the Bank of England. It is not only readers with a penchant for nostalgia who will look moist-eyed on the statistic that, with the exception of two tiny differences in late 1939, bank rate remained constant at the now almost unbelievably low level of 2 per cent between June 1932 and October 1951.

See **minimum lending rate** for further discussion

base rate
In banking, the starting point for a bank's calculations of its interest rates. Where the rates on its **deposit accounts** are concerned, the same rates of interest will apply to all holders of such accounts. With the interest that the bank will charge on **loans** and **overdrafts**, however, it is up to individual customers to obtain the best deal they can. Branch managers have a fair amount of discretion in these matters, and will take into consideration the risk involved, the customer's standing and influence, etc. When this rate is agreed, it will often be quoted in terms of so many per cent above base rate. Thus, with a base rate of 14 per cent, if a customer is to be charged 18 per cent the agreement may stipulate that interest will be at a level of '4 per cent above base rate'. The actual rate will then vary directly with any movements in the base.

See also **turn**

batch
In banking, a number of **credit** items and the corresponding **debit** items **listed** to ensure that the totals of each agree. *Batch*

has its origins in Anglo-Saxon *bacan* 'to bake', a batch being the outcome of a single baking. It is now of wide application—for example, we can speak of a batch of books, parcels or correspondence—and the banker's use of the term is basically no different. However, its meaning is often extended into a quite specialized area: it can be used as a shorthand synonym for the *process* of **listing** and agreeing items on **batch sheets**. If a credit or cheque somehow manages to reach the section of the branch that is responsible for items being **posted** to customers' accounts without having first passed through this listing, a superior may well demand to know why it has not 'been through the batch'. It is the grammatical construction using the definite article which produces the extension of meaning: a newcomer to banking would use *a batch*, expecting *the batch* to refer to a specified set of items; only an experienced banker would use *the batch* to mean the process. (Interestingly enough in this context, the *Oxford English Dictionary* gives 'the process of baking' as an obsolete meaning of *batch*.)

With the ever-increasing tendency for banks to remove as much as possible of the tedious 'bookkeeping' aspects of their work to centres outside the branches, leaving staff free to liaise with customers, the system described above is currently disappearing.

batch sheet

In banking, a sheet of paper on which a **batch** is **listed**. Alternative terms are *remittance sheet* (the relevant section of the branch being itself known as *Remittances* or, colloquially, as *Rems*), *control sheet*, *proof sheet* and *waste sheet*. Accordingly, banks variously refer to this part of branch banking as **proving**, **control** and, most interestingly, as **waste**. However, the probable disappearance of all this terminology is mentioned in the final paragraph of the preceding entry.

best advice

In banking, building societies and life assurance, advice given by an **agent**, acting for only one company, or by an **independent financial adviser**. The agent is obliged to recommend only the best of that company's **products**, with the additional proviso that, should the company not have a suitable product, this must be made clear. An independent financial adviser, on the other hand, must select from what the adviser believes to be the best available from all providers.

bill

In banking, short for **bills of exchange**, a method of payment now largely superseded by cheques for settlement of inland commercial debts, although still widely used in foreign trade. To be accurate, a cheque is simply a special kind of bill: it is defined by Section 73 of the Bills of Exchange Act, 1882 as 'a bill of exchange drawn on a banker payable on demand'. *Bill* may be an especially misleading term, as it will be already known to English speakers as a word having two different financial senses, neither of which is intended here: to users of British English as a synonym for *invoice* or *account rendered*, and to Americans as their word for paper money, eg a *10-dollar bill*.

See also **foreign bill**

bill of exchange

See **bill**

bin

In banking and building societies, the receptacle that collects **captured cards** in an **automated teller machine**.

bin number

In banking and building societies, a code number allocated to an item of stationery, used with reference to items within branches, especially when re-ordering them from the institutions' stationery departments. It presumably takes its name from the fact that items are stored in bulk in these departments in partitioned stands, just as vintners store bottles of wine in 'bins'. The term is quite widespread in other areas of commerce: many department stores, for example, refer to the shelves in their stockrooms as *bins*, the items of merchandise having *bin numbers*, and the process of piling them on the shelves being known as *binning*.

black list

In banking, a list of the names of customers whose accounts are so unsatisfactory that **cashiers** are instructed to check the balances and, if necessary, refer the matter to a higher authority before cashing cheques. Black lists are, of course, in use in many other areas of life: the *Oxford English Dictionary* traces an example of its use as 'a list of persons who have incurred suspicion, censure or punishment' back to 1619. In some branches, the cashiers refer to such lists as *trigger lists*, because their function is to set in motion the process of enquiry into the state of a particular customer's account. Additionally, some branches maintain, by obvious analogy, a *grey list* of customers whose accounts may be troublesome but who do not warrant adding to the black list.

Although *black list* (together with *grey list*) remains by far the most common name for the document concerned, there are moves afoot, via the courses mounted in the banks for new cashiers, to encourage the use of *reference list* or *customer refer list* or *counter refer list* instead. This is not a matter of euphemism alone. Customers overhearing one cashier telling another to 'put Mary Brown on the reference list' would be much less likely to realize that they had eavesdropped on privileged information than if *black list* had been used.

The newer terms take their names from the expression *refer the cheque*. When cashiers go behind the scenes to check on the state of customers' accounts, they are said to be *referring the cheques*, which may involve simply confirming that there are sufficient **funds** in the account or, if there are not, obtaining authority from the manager before paying out the cash.

Incidentally, banks have always taken care to minimize the risk of actions for libel by deliberately having the lists typed without a heading or title of any kind.

See also **colour terms** and **in the red**

blue
See **colour terms**

BM

In building societies, an abbreviation sometimes used by clerks for **borrowing member**. The term appears to be in the process of widening its area of meaning: etymologically, it refers only to those taking out **loans**, but it is now increasingly being used to refer to any customer. Thus, a memorandum within the office might give a customer's name and address, with the note 'BM requires balance on Deposit Account No . . .'

bonus

In life assurance, an additional sum of money payable on **maturity** to the holder of a with profits policy (see **assurance**). Its size will depend on the investment expertise of the company.

BOWS and FOWS

/ˈbaʊz n ˈfaʊz/ In building societies, a short form of **Back Office Workstations and Front Office Workstations**—not quite on a par with **secs and recs**, but quite appealing to the ear nonetheless. A workstation here normally takes the form of a computer keyboard, monitor, and printer, whilst the back office and front office allusions are to whether these pieces of technology are located behind the scenes or by the **cashiers** at the counter. If an electrical failure brings them all to a halt, one may hear the complaint that 'all the BOWS and FOWS are down'.

branch cheque

In banking, not a cheque at all, strictly speaking, but a **draft** drawn by a bank branch against its own account.

See **banker's draft**

branch clearing

In banking, cheques accepted by a branch of a **collecting bank**, drawn on other branches of that same bank, and grouped together for transmission through the **clearing**.

See also **general clearing**

bridging loan

In banking and building societies, a loan made by an institution (usually a bank) to 'bridge' the gap that householders can otherwise fall into between having to pay for a new house and receiving the **proceeds** of the sale of the old one. It is often made available in the form of an **overdraft** on a customer's **current account**.

broker

See **brokerage**

brokerage

In building societies, a percentage payment to a professional (solicitor, accountant, etc) who directs **funds** to a building society for a useful length of time; also known as *commission*. Professionals who acquire a reputation for **hot money** (not in the criminal sense) do not receive such payments, and are known as *non-brokerage* or *non-commission connections*. The term also operates in a wider sense, referring to the charge levied by *brokers* of various kinds, such as insurance brokers, for their services as intermediaries between companies and clients. *Broker* comes from Old French *brochier* 'to broach (ie pierce) a barrel'—the connection being that the *broachers* would then retail the wine, thereby functioning as intermediaries between producers and consumers.

bullion

In banks and building societies, widely, bulk amounts of cash, such as those delivered or taken periodically by security companies. Gold or silver ingots are probably what come to mind when bullion is mentioned to the general public: its etymology via the Old French *bouillir* — 'to boil' links with the 'ordinary' sense of bars produced by a process of melting down metal. However, the term is not used consistently throughout the institutions. In one, 'They're coming to take our bullion this afternoon' refers to surplus notes and coin (ie paper as well as metal money); whilst in another, with the word sticking a little closer to its origins, 'We'll have to check the bullion in the safe' denotes coin only.

buy high, sell low

In banking, a maxim of the **foreign clerk** when dealing with currencies. It is the way in which most currencies are quoted in Britain—one pound sterling to a varying number of foreign units, and not the other way round—which accounts for this seemingly strange advice.

Foreign currency dealers, like traders in any other commodity, make their living by buying at one price and selling at another; and in applying the motto 'buy high, sell low', the clerk is merely operating the same principle as a market stallholder who buys oranges at eight for 90 pence and sells them at five for 90 pence.

C

cancel

In banking, to indicate that a cheque is **in order** by a bank official superimposing his or her initials on the **drawer's** signature. The public may find this a confusing usage: customers are known to talk about having *cancelled* a cheque when they have stopped payment of it, or have destroyed one that has been drawn in error (see **answer** for further discussion of these two contingencies). To a banker, however, cancelling a cheque is the process of indicating that there are no **technical irregularities**, that the drawer's signature is genuine, and so on. In small branches, this task may be performed by one or two **cashiers**; in a large city bank, it may be spread among a dozen or more, supervised by a *chief canceller*. (All that said, it must be added that the practice of cancelling every cheque which comes into a branch is, like so many other time-consuming clerical tasks, disappearing. Banks seem to be taking the view that it is better to run the risk of, for example, paying an out-of-date cheque and eventually having to reimburse the customer than to spend many hours of staff time away from customers on a duty which, for the most part, consists of confirming that everything is the way it is supposed to be.)

If a cheque which has been received in a morning's clearing and cancelled in fact has to be returned unpaid (for example, the drawer stops payment of it during the course of the day), then in addition to the relevant answer, the cheque will be sent back bearing the legend *Cancelled in error*.

We may, perhaps, reflect on the formality of all this. *Cancelled* is precisely the word used in Section 63 of the Bills of Exchange Act of 1882: 'Where a bill is intentionally cancelled . . . and the cancellation is apparent thereon . . .'. This formality both reflects and focuses the banker's attention on the seriousness of the situation. If an error is not noticed in time, cancelling a cheque which should not have been paid can have very serious repercussions. The retention of a highly formal word for the action is a powerful factor in preventing flippant attitudes towards the action itself.

See Appendix 2 for a fuller discussion of the functions of financial terminology.

cancelled in error
See **cancel**

captured card
In banking and building societies, a cashcard retained by a cash-dispensing machine. As many customers know, an **automated teller machine** does not always return their plastic cards. A card may be retained for one or more of a number of reasons—for example, the card may be stolen or damaged, the customer may have failed to enter the correct **personal identification number**, or the card may not have been taken back by the user from the machine within a specified time (cf. **time out**). It will end up in the **bin**.

CAR
See **compounded annual rate**

case
In life assurance, a **proposal** that has been submitted by a branch of a life assurance company to its head office, or the name of the customer concerned. A telephone query from the head office to the branch might begin, 'This case of yours, a Mrs Green . . .'.

cashcard
See **plastic**

cash dispenser
See **automated teller machine**

cashier
In banks and building societies, a member of branch staff who receives and pays out money (not necessarily cash); the US

equivalent is **teller**. In building societies especially, cashiers may have far wider responsibilities for guiding customers through the maze of accounts and other **products**, and hence may acquire titles such as *Financial Services Advisers* instead.

cast

In banks and building societies, to add up a set of figures to produce a total; also, the total so obtained. When banking and building-society staff talk about *casting the books*, they are employing a term that the *Oxford English Dictionary* records as having been in use among those concerned with accounts since the early fourteenth century.

Two derived terms are worthy of mention. The first is the verb to *short cast*. Although the activity is much less common with the spread of pocket calculators and other electronic aids, some members of staff prefer not to wait until the bottom of a column or the end of an accounting period has been reached to cast the figures, but to take advantage of a slack period and add them up to that point, usually entering the resulting sub-total in pencil or a differently coloured ink. Thus, a clerk who balances an account in a seemingly amazingly quick time may explain, 'Ah, but I'd short cast it just five minutes before the final entry'.

The second is also a verb, to *cross-cast*. This is the process of adding figures in both rows and columns. If all the sums are correct, the grand total of the figures at the foot of the columns will be the same as that of those at the end of the rows. The truth of this can be checked from the following highly simplified table, showing a grand total of £900 in the bottom right-hand box:

	Jan	Feb	Mar	Totals
	£	£	£	£
Postage	100	110	120	330
Stationery	220	180	170	570
Totals	320	290	290	900

charge

In banking, building societies and life assurance, as in general usage, payment due for service rendered. For example, lots of people resent paying **bank charges**. However, this use needs to be carefully distinguished from that intended in connection with **security** for a **loan**. If your bank says that it wants to 'take a charge' on your life assurance policy, it is not referring to a financial cost. Instead, the plan is for the bank to ask you to **assign** the policy to them, giving them certain rights over it, most importantly the right to repay the loan from the **proceeds** of the policy, if need be.

chief canceller

See **cancel**

child's guide

In banking, a binder containing guides to the application of Exchange Control Regulations, now obsolete. Bankers are not above a little tongue-in-cheek flippancy. In the days of control of transactions outside what was known as the Sterling Area, branches would, from time to time, receive amendments and additions to the existing directives from the Bank of England. As these had the force of law, they were couched in legal and quasi-legal terminology, and consequently were often less than immediately comprehensible to those who had to act upon them. For this reason, the binder holding the instructions (at least in some bank branches) was ironically known as the *child's guide*.

The phrase, presumably formed by analogy with *child's play*, regrettably appears to have been ephemeral. It is seemingly unrecorded in dictionaries, and, with the abolition of Exchange Control Regulations in Britain, the binder has disappeared and its sobriquet with it.

clearance

In banking, payment of a cheque that has been transmitted through the **clearing**.

clearer

In banking, a bank that is a member of the London **clearing house**. It is only during the last 30 years or so that *clearer* has been used in the sense of *clearing bank*. The *Oxford English Dictionary*'s citation from the 1883 *Bankers Magazine* shows that it was originally used for the people actually effecting the **clearing**: 'The men who transact the clearing business for the various banks are called *the clearers*.' Today, the term is primarily a journalistic one, bankers themselves preferring the more formal *clearing banks*.

clearing

In banking, the process of obtaining **clearance**; also, the actual cheques that are sent or received for clearance. The term is in use among all banks. The London Bankers' **clearing house** provides facilities for the exchange of cheques drawn on branches of all the principal commercial banks, so that cheques credited to beneficiaries' accounts are **presented** to the drawers' branches for payment, usually within three working days. The actual transfer of funds is handled, with the use of computers, by the Bankers' Automated Clearing Services (BACS). The cheques that arrive at branches each morning are themselves referred to as the *clearing* (cf. the metaphorical processes affecting **pipeline** in building-society use), or, where more precision is required, as the *in-clearing*. One example from the *Oxford English Dictionary* beautifully encompasses three items of interest (*house*, *drafts* and *clearing*): 1827: the drafts which are drawn upon the house, and which have come in from the clearing . . . are called the 'clearing in'. The first true example of *in-clearing* is dated at 1878, and follows the pattern of verbal nouns such as *in-gathering* and *in-fetching*, formed by prefixing the adverbial *in* to a present participle. The *out-clearing* is the parcel of cheques which have been paid in at a branch during the day to be sent for collection (see **collecting bank**) via the clearing house.

Because this sense of *clearing* is not restricted to any one bank, and also because it is used in related senses by other (non-financial) institutions, there is a tendency for banks to use it in conversation or correspondence with their customers. However, it seems probable that its precise meaning in context is not always readily retrievable by the receiver. Where a customer is not too happy about the worth of a cheque he or she has paid in, an enquiry is often made of the **cashier** on the following day to see if it has been paid or returned. The banker will normally reply that it is too soon to know 'because the cheque is still in the clearing'. One banker's reflection on his own habit of responding in this way was, 'I often wonder afterwards just how much sense it made to the customer.'

clearing house

In banking, an establishment providing facilities for the exchange of cheques and other items between **collecting banks** and **paying banks**. In *clearing house*, bankers can claim to have coined a useful phrase. The London Bankers' clearing house was established in 1775, but by the mid-nineteenth century the term had been borrowed to describe other institutions dealing in a similar way with quite different matters. The *Oxford English Dictionary* records 'The London Clearing-House is enabled to trace the course of all waggons and passenger-carriages' (1849) as merely one example, and before the end of that century *Harper's Magazine* (September 1883) was able to use the term figuratively to say that 'The Charity Organization Society is a central exchange or clearing house for all the single relief associations.'

collateral (security)

In banking and building societies, a phrase sometimes used by customers (who may have picked it up from American films and TV series) to mean almost any type of **security**. To British lenders, however, it specifically contrasts with **direct security** (property owned by the borrower personally). Collateral (security), as its name (='by the side') suggests, is security provided by a third party whose actions run parallel to the main transaction. So, if poor daughter A borrows money from kind banker B, rich father C may be asked to provide a guarantee as collateral, indicating that, if his offspring does not repay the loan, he will.

The careful distinction between *direct security* and *collateral* may be disappearing. A booklet issued for the guidance of borrowers from one major building society refers to 'the collateral provided by the property'.

collecting bank

In banking, a bank that accepts cheques for **credit** to its customers' accounts and passes them through the **clearing** to obtain payment of them from the banks on which they are drawn; compare **paying bank**. Just how close the language of banking can border on the esoteric may be judged from the following specimen letter offered as a model to bankers in a textbook published in 1948 (A & E E Fieldhouse, *The Student's Theory and Practice of Commerce*):

> We have to inform you that a cheque for £50, drawn by Messrs. Jones & Robinson, on the Yorkshire Banking Co., Ltd., in your favour, and handed to us for collection, has been returned marked R/D [return to drawer].
>
> Herewith we return Cheque, the amount of which has been debited to your account.

The public could be forgiven for being puzzled by the thought of someone being handed a cheque and that person then being asked to collect it. Even if they (correctly) work out that this is a shorthand way of referring not to the cheque itself but to the sum it represents, they might still erroneously conclude that the person entrusted with the cheque was being sent to obtain hard cash in place of the piece of paper. In fact, only those conversant with banking terminology would know that, when a cheque is paid into a bank account, that bank becomes a *collecting bank*, charged with the responsibility of ensuring that the cheque goes through the system and arrives at the *drawee bank* (the **paying bank**). Even then, the transfer of **funds** is effected by 'book entries'—no actual cash changes hands. All banks, of course, normally act as both collecting and paying banks throughout the day.

colour terms

In banking, words used as a means of reference to documents printed on a particular colour of paper or to books with significantly coloured covers. In one bank, a *blue* refers to a diary note, such as an account of an interview with a customer at which an **overdraft** was agreed, detailing amount, period of indebtedness, etc. A copy of this, known as a *green*, would be deposited in the file of the customer concerned. In another bank, however, a *green* indicates something completely different, namely, the Cash Order Form on which a branch records its weekly cash requirements from its local centre. When such cash arrives, it is accompanied by a Cash Transmission Form, but it is most improbable that anyone involved in the transfer will refer to it by this title. The receiving **cashier** is much more likely to ask simply, 'Have you got the pink (form)?'

It is not single documents alone that take their colloquial names from their distinctive colours. A book, too, sometimes acquires a sobriquet derived from the colour of its binding: the *Cash To and From Safe Book* is invariably alluded to in one bank merely as the *green book*, while the *grey book* is properly the *Foreign Instruction Manual*, which provides guidance for the benefit of clerks in the bank's foreign departments, and the *white book* is really the *Securities from Safe Book*, whose title is self-explanatory.

Why these pseudonyms should be employed rather than abbreviations is difficult to say. Certainly there are precedents: the *Oxford English Dictionary* gives examples of *blue book* in various contexts dating back over three centuries, and economists in particular use *Blue Book* to refer to the detailed account of national income and expenditure published by the British government in August or September each year.

It may be a matter of brevity—the *Cash To and From Safe Book* is rendered even more quickly in speech as the *green book* than it would be as the *CTFS book*. Against this, however, one has to set the rejected possibility of acronyms—*FIM* for *Foreign Instruction Manual* and *COF* for *Cash Order Form*. Surely someone must have found the idea of the punning 'Have you got a COF /kɒf/ ?' irresistible. And perhaps, as so often, therein lies the answer: because the seriousness of the commodity in which bankers deal has to remain unquestionable, any hint of humour in reference to it is studiously avoided.

See Appendix 2 for a fuller discussion of the functions of financial terminology.

commission
See **brokerage**

composite rate tax
A form of income tax in the UK which, until recently, banks and building societies were obliged to deduct from the interest credited to their customers' accounts (see **net** and **gross**). As this was levied on all accounts regardless of the

customers' tax statuses, it meant that governments received tax from those who were not otherwise liable to pay it (such as large numbers of children and pensioners) and who were not permitted to reclaim it. To offset this effect, the level was set at a rate below standard rate so that, for example, with basic rate tax at 25 per cent, composite rate tax was only 22 per cent. Not unreasonably, those with a low income who were effectively subsidizing those with a higher income felt this to be a less than equitable arrangement. The composite rate tax scheme was abolished with effect from 6 April 1991, and replaced with a fairer system whereby taxpayers continue to have tax deducted from their interest but at basic rate, whilst non-taxpayers are able to self-certify their tax status and receive their interest **gross**.

compounded annual rate (CAR)

/si: eɪ ɑ:ʳ/ In building societies, an interest rate which incorporates in its calculation the fact that interest is applied more than once a year. Interest is thus paid on interest as well as on capital. In order to give the most accurate indication of the interest to be earned on their investment accounts (and, of course, to present them in the best possible light) many building societies now show a **net** CAR. Thus, an ordinary net rate of 11 per cent per annum will be shown as having an equivalent CAR of 11.30 per cent. The basis of this conversion is that, whilst the 11 per cent is an annual rate, the interest is in fact credited to the account every six months. Assuming no other transactions on the account, therefore, a typical set of calculations would be as follows:

		£
1 January	Deposit	10 000.00
30 June	6 months' interest @ 11 per cent per annum	550.00
	New balance	10 550.00
31 December	6 months' interest @ 11 per cent per annum	580.25
	New balance	11 130.25

In whole pounds, then, interest of £1130, rather than £1100, has been earned on the £10 000, giving a true rate of 11.30 per cent rather than 11.00 per cent.

control

In banking and building societies, a term with many meanings: in some banks, the section of a branch which processes **batches**; in others, the section which deals with opening and closing accounts, changing details on customers' files, etc. In some building societies, the term functions as an approximate equivalent of *chief cashier* (see **cashier**).

control sheet

In life assurance, a form listing all the information concerning a **proposal** (name, age, medical history, etc) before these facts are put onto the computer. As in its banking sense, therefore (compare **batch sheet**), the reference is to an initial, temporary record which is quickly superseded by a more permanent one.

correct

In banking, used in the everyday sense of 'amend', but more particularly used as a coded device for asking customers to maintain their affairs in accordance with agreements. If you receive a letter from your bank which mentions *correcting*, it is possible that it is referring to putting right an error. Rather more probable, unfortunately, is a context such as 'Your current account is now overdrawn to the extent of £*x*,' where the accompanying request to 'correct the situation' is a polite way of asking you either to restore a **credit** balance or at least to come back to within the agreed overdraft **limit**. *Regularize the position* functions as a synonymous phrase.

See also **in order**

correspondence clerk

In banking, as the name suggests, one whose duties include handling items of general correspondence. Whilst this 'full' term is generally used in conversation with customers, *Corres* /'kɒrɛz/ is much more prevalent in informal notes or in speech behind the counter.

counterfoil

In banking and building societies, usually a small slip of paper providing details of the record of a cheque, paying-in slip, etc, which is detached then retained by the customer. Cheque counterfoils in particular are often colloquially referred to as *stubs*, whilst *counterfoil* itself has replaced **memorandum** in relation to paying-in slips.

countermanded

See **answer**

counter refer list

See **black list**

country

In banking, cheques drawn on branches anywhere in England other than London, which is *Town*. The *Oxford English Dictionary* traces this dichotomy back to 1593, citing Thomas Nashe's *Christ's Teares over Jerusalem*: 'In the Country, the Gentleman ... undoeth the Farmer. In London, the Vsurer snatcheth up the Gentleman'.

See also **country notes**

country notes

In banking, banknotes previously issued by banks outside the City of London. Early banking companies formed of a maximum of six people were allowed to issue their own notes. During the eighteenth century the London private banks encouraged the use of cheques in place of their own notes, which they eventually stopped using altogether, leaving Bank of England notes as the only ones issued in London. However, hundreds of new banks were formed in industrial areas, each issuing its own notes. Reference is made under the entry for **country** to the practice of alluding to all banks outside the City as *country banks*; their notes, similarly, became known as **country notes**. The commercial banks in Scotland and Ireland, it should be remembered, still retain their right to note-issue, so that on present-day paying-in slips the *country notes* section has been replaced by one marked *S & I*, ie **Scotch and Irish**.

cr

The abbreviation for **credit**.

See **dr** for its etymology

credit

In banking, building societies, and life assurance, a sum of money paid into a customer's account, or a **voucher** representing this amount. The term is also used as a verb, to enter this sum in an account.

See also **debit**

credit open (or **credit opened**)

In banking, an arrangement whereby a customer's branch authorizes another branch or bank to cash that customer's cheques up to a specified limit within a given period. The increased use of cheque cards, which currently guarantee cheques usually to a maximum of £50, and the spread of **automated teller machines** (cash dispensers) have led to a diminished demand for credits open(ed), but they have by no means disappeared.

cross

See **crossing**

cross cast

See **cast**

crossed cheque

See **crossing**

cross-fire

See **answer**

crossing

In banking, two parallel lines drawn across the face of a cheque. These may be inserted by a customer on what is originally an **open cheque**, or they may be already provided by the printer so that the customer has a book of *crossed cheques*.

And Co or *& Co* are often added, but these are superfluous and have no effect. Section 76 of the 1882 Bills of Exchange Act specifies that 'The words *and company* or any abbreviation thereof between two parallel transverse lines' may appear, or 'two parallel transverse lines only'. The result of crossing a cheque is that it must be paid into a bank account—it cannot (ordinarily) be cashed over the counter. It is possible for a **drawer** to *open the crossing* by writing and signing instructions to that effect between the lines, but banks are rightly suspicious of such *openings*.

Two additions to crossings are worth special mention. The first is the phrase *account payee* (sometimes with the word *only* suffixed). Although this has no statutory force, a **collecting bank** which accepted a cheque so marked for the credit of an account other than that of the **payee** would be acting very unwisely and probably negligently.

The second is *not negotiable*, which often worries payees, especially those who do not have bank accounts of their own and who wish to ask a friend or local trader to cash a cheque bearing these words, and who mistakenly think that the expression is equivalent to *not transferable*. In fact, the transferability of the cheque is not affected at all. What is changed is the ability to pass on what the lawyer refers to as *title*, which in this case means the right to the money: the holder of a *not negotiable* cheque cannot pass on a better title than that possessed by the holder.

Thus: Mary writes out a cheque payable to John; Peter steals the cheque, forges John's signature on the back of the cheque and persuades James to give him cash for it. If the cheque bears only an ordinary crossing, there is little that anyone can do. However, if the cheque has been crossed *not negotiable*, no one who takes the cheque following the thief's signature (eg James or his bank) can have a good title to it, and it should be possible to reclaim the money from them.

currency notes

In banking, £1 and 10-shilling notes, issued by the Treasury at the start of World War 1, and not to be confused with present-day foreign currency notes. In 1928, the Currency and Bank Notes Act enabled the Bank of England to take over responsibility for currency notes, which were then deemed to be bank notes alongside the higher value ones already in issue. Incidentally, the largest value notes ever in circulation in Britain were for £1000, withdrawn in 1943.

current account

In banking and building societies, a type of account once offered only by banks but now increasingly available from building societies as well. It provides not only a cheque book but also access to a full range of facilities—**overdrafts**, **standing orders**, **direct debits**, etc—not normally given to holders of other types of accounts.

customer refer list

See **black list**

D

death in service

In life assurance, an agreed sum paid by a life assurance company where a person dies in the service of a firm. This benefit is usually incorporated in an arranged pension scheme, but provides cover prior to retirement.

debit

In banking, building societies and life assurance, a sum of money paid out of a customer's account, or a **voucher** representing this sum. The term is also used as a verb, meaning to enter this sum in an account. It is the opposite of **credit**.

There are several standard letters issued by banks today to deal with the situation where a cheque which has been paid into an account has been returned unpaid and cannot be immediately **presented** again. A frequent formula is 'The cheque is enclosed and the amount of £x has been debited to your account'.

Trainee bookkeepers in commercial enterprises are taught to 'debit value in, credit value out'. For example, if Company A sells goods to Company B on the understanding that B will pay at the end of the month, A will credit its sales account (goods having gone out) and debit B's account (B having received something valuable, namely, the goods). The logic of this becomes clearer if it is realized that B has become A's debtor. Unfortunately, having firmly established knowledge of this routine in one's mind, one then has to recognize that the banker lives through the looking-glass, where the commercial bookkeeper's debits and credits are completely reversed. This is not sheer bloody-mindedness, no matter what first-year bookkeeping students may think; it is accounted for by the fact that banks see depositors as people who lend them money.

When, therefore, the recipient of a standard letter originally paid in the cheque for £x, the bank would have placed it to the *credit* of that person's account, ie the payee would have been the bank's creditor for that sum. By the same token, when it became necessary for it to be removed from the account, this was achieved by *debiting* it.

decreasing term assurance
See **term assurance**

deed box
In banking, a generic title for any kind of lockable container in which customers place items to leave them in **safe custody**. As the key is retained by the customer, the contents of the box are unknown to the bank, and the receipt for the box normally bears words to that effect, but it is probably only a minority that contain actual deeds. The deeds of most customers' properties are held as **security** by their mortgagees (see **mortgage**), and these containers are frequently used to store other valuable documents such as insurance policies and share certificates.

deposit account
1 In banking, the basic type of account on offer to savers, with a rate of interest usually several percentage points below the particular bank's **base rate**. Although treated by most customers as being accounts where their savings are freely available on demand, technically seven days' notice of withdrawal is required. What actually happens—although relatively few deposit account holders are aware of it—is that the bank allows withdrawals without the need for notice, but deducts seven days' interest, on the amount withdrawn, when it calculates the sum to be credited periodically.

2 In building societies, an account which offers rather less interest than the normal **share account**. A compensating advantage is that, in the event of a society being wound up, depositors (as opposed to other types of savers) would have prior claim on the society's assets. Reasonably enough, given the stability of the building society movement, not many customers view this with much concern, with the result that there is no great take-up of these accounts by the public.

difference

In banking and building societies, the discrepancy between two sides of an account that should **balance**. If, by mishap, they fail to do so, it is not because anything so common as a *mistake* has been made. The bank (and building society) cashier's term is the nicely euphemistic *difference*, so that one cashier will ask of a frustrated colleague, 'How much is your difference?'

British bookkeepers are not alone in this. Moufflet, writing in 1956 of the language of French administration in *Vie et Langage*, had this to say:

Une figure de rhétorique couramment utilisée dans l'Administration est euphémisme. Par exemple, dans les services de comptabilité, on ne parlera jamais d'erreur, mais de *différence*. 'Une différence a été constatée dans les écritures du bureau des Fonds et Liquidations.'

[Euphemism is a commonly used figure of speech in administration. For example, in accounts departments, one never speaks of an *error* but of a *difference*. 'A difference has been discovered in the accounts of the Funds and Liquidations Office.']

direct debit

In banking, a regular payment made under a system whereby the beneficiary initiates the transaction (after, of course, the receipt by the bank of signed instructions from its customer). Whereas with a **banker's order** the bank **debits** its customer's account and subsequently passes a corresponding **credit** through the system until it reaches the beneficiary's account, with a direct debit the beneficiary produces (or at least originally produced) a **voucher** that finds its way through the **clearing** process to be debited to the customer. The net result, of course, is exactly the same in both cases, and as both procedures employ the banks' clearing services, the term *direct* is something of a misnomer. With the increased computerization of the procedure, the nomenclature will almost certainly become more accurate: already, the 'voucher' is in reality no more than an entry on a printout (see **truncation**).

direct security

In banks and building societies, property which is deposited as **security** for a loan by the borrower personally. Examples include a life **assurance** policy in which the borrower is the **life assured** and beneficiary, or a share certificate in the borrower's own name. *Direct security* contrasts with **collateral security**.

discount

See **premium**

dishonour

In banking, to refuse to pay a cheque, returning it unpaid with a particular **answer**.

dividend mandate

See **mandate**

doc credit

See **documentary credit**

documentary credit

In banking, an arrangement enabling exporters to obtain payment for their goods. Where exporters are shipping goods to new customers, or to customers whose financial status may otherwise be in doubt, they may be reluctant to employ the normal procedure of drawing a **foreign bill**. In such cases, it is common for a documentary credit (normally referred to by a banker as a *doc credit*) to be set up. This involves the importer's bank lending its name (in place of the importer's) as the **drawee** of the **bill**, and on the shipping documents accompanying the foreign bill. Naturally, the foreign bank will release the documents to its customer, giving access to the goods, only if it is satisfied that it will be reimbursed for paying the foreign bill. *Credit* appears in a related sense in domestic banking in **credit open**.

down

See **lock out**

dr

In banking, building societies and life assurance, the abbreviation for **debit**. This word has an interesting etymology. In the fifteenth to seventeenth centuries, the left-hand side of a bookkeeper's accounts was headed *Debitor*, which subsequently gave way to *Debtor*, abbreviated to *Dr*. As the items entered on this side were (and still are) *debits*, it became common during the nineteenth century to refer to the *debit side* rather than the *debtor side*. The abbreviation *Dr* being long-established by then, it remained in use after its original full form had disappeared, with its meaning simply transferred from the older to the newer attributive.

Creditor, *credit* and *Cr* have a parallel history: *Cr* is an abbreviation formed from the initial and final letters of *creditor*, and not, as one might otherwise have been tempted to guess, from the first two of *credit*.

draft

In banking, broadly, any written order to pay a sum of money; occasionally used as an abbreviation for **banker's draft**; also, a cheque drawn in a foreign currency at a customer's request. This happens where, for example, an inhabitant of Britain wishes to subscribe to an American journal and payment is required in US dollars. In this case, therefore, a draft is substituted for a personal cheque, not so much because of lack of certainty of the subscriber's financial standing, but because a cheque issued directly by the subscriber would be drawn in what would be, to the recipient, a foreign currency.

draw

In banking, to write a cheque or, less commonly, any other type of **bill** of exchange.

drawee

In banking, the person on whom a **bill** of exchange is drawn, ie the debtor in a transaction. In the case of a cheque, which is simply a special kind of bill of exchange, this 'person' is always a bank.

drawee bank

See **paying bank**

drawer

In banking, the signatory to a cheque—the name of the account on which a cheque is **drawn**. For *refer to drawer*, see **answer**.

dynamic pensions

See **dynamize**

dynamize

In life assurance, to increase pension payments at agreed intervals, more commonly referred to as *escalate* (or, quite simply, *increase*). One company, however—the Provident Mutual Life Assurance Association—has, for the last 30 years, been using a quite different word in this context, with its reference to *dynamic pensions*, suitably implying the movement and growth which are the important features of such **products**. This life **office** may justly claim to have introduced a family of terms which has been found readily usable by quite different bodies who have an interest in pension schemes. By 1969, the then Department of Health and Social Security had taken up the terms for use in White Papers (Cmnd 3883, January and Cmnd 4195, November), where one finds, in addition to *dynamic pensions*, a *dynamic element* and an *undynamized abatement system*. Similarly, in the 'Practice Notes' issued by the Inland Revenue in 1979, there are references to *dynamized final remuneration* and to sums expressed *without any dynamism*.

It would be going too far to suggest that the Provident Mutual was the originator of *dynamize*: the *Oxford English Dictionary* records it, in the sense of 'increase the power of medicines', as being in use since 1855. However, the word and its related forms have definitely been given a new lease of life by their extension into fresh fields. Perhaps it would be both fair and fitting to say that the Provident Mutual has dynamized them?

E

easy

In banking and building societies, applied to **mortgage funds** in ready supply. *Easy* and **tight** are opposites used by financiers in relation to the supply of money in general, so that it is not surprising to be told by a branch official of a building society that, 'With monthly **quotas** being easier, we don't get as much aggravation from head office. When money's really tight, we get memos on a monthly basis.'

economy plan policy

In life assurance, a policy which provides assurance/insurance cover for a low **premium**. For a discussion of the use of euphemism in the life assurance business, see **life assured**.

effects (not cleared)

See **answer**

either signature to operate

See **ESTO**

endorse

In banking, to write on the back of a document; less frequently, **indorse**. Although, legally, there are various ways in which one can endorse a cheque or other **bill** of exchange, easily the most common is the simple device of signing one's name on the back—exactly as the word's etymology ('put on back') suggests. A cheque endorsed in this fashion (technically, *in blank*) becomes payable to bearer. One occasionally hears shopkeepers who are cashing cheques for customers who lack accounts of their own employing an Anglo-Saxon version of *endorse*: 'Just back the cheque for me, would you?'

endowment assurance

See **assurance**

endowment mortgage

In banking, building societies and life assurance, one of the two most common types of **mortgage**, where the borrower repays only the interest on the loan during its term. The capital sum is repaid from the **proceeds** of a life **assurance** policy taken out at the same time as the mortgage is effected. This arrangement is popular, even now when tax relief on new life assurance **premiums** has been abolished in the UK, because it is often possible for a borrower to pay no more in combined interest and premiums than would have been paid in capital and interest under a **repayment mortgage**, but be left with a substantial sum in profits and bonuses after the loan has been repaid on maturity of the policy.

equity

In banking and building societies, the net value of a property to its owner, ie the total value less the sum outstanding on a **mortgage** loan; also, in wider usage, an ordinary share in a company.

The interplay between mortgagees and professions working in related areas is shown in their use of this term. As with *debit* and *credit*, we must first turn to accounting practices for the basis of an explanation. A traditional balance sheet had two sides: the *assets*, listing premises, goods, cash, etc—all the things owned by a business (including debts owed to it); and the *liabilities*, showing sums owed by the business. The balancing item on the liabilities side represented the capital invested in the business by the owner(s)—its *net worth*. In other words, if the business went into liquidation, all assets were converted into cash and all debts to outsiders were paid off, the sum remaining would be the net worth of the business to the owner(s). Now, in the case of a limited company, the owners hold shares, and it has become the practice to refer to the net value of a company to its ordinary shareholders as the *equity*. By extension, the ordinary shares have become known as *equities*, so that the financial press carries reports such as 'Equities stay firm ahead of trade figures' and 'The equity market went into decline.'

The reasons behind this choice of word are logical enough. After a liquidated company has paid all its creditors and preference shareholders, the remaining cash, if any, is shared equitably among the ordinary shareholders, ie each share attracts an equal amount. Similar considerations apply to the distribution of profits while a company continues to trade.

The *Oxford English Dictionary* indicates that this use of *equity* originated in the USA, where it has the wider sense of the value to all its owners other than those with an external interest. It is in this sense, ie the owner's share, that it has been taken over by both American and British mortgagees. The biggest investment in the lives of average citizens is in their own houses, and for most of those citizens a mortgage loan is required. As with a limited company, therefore, there is frequently an outside party with a financial interest. By analogy, then, the net value of the property to its owner is referred to as the *equity*. So, if a house is valued at £40 000 and there is an outstanding mortgage of £30 000, a bank or building society manager would refer to the fact that 'the equity is £10 000' or that 'the owners have a 25 per cent equity in their house'.

Bank managers and solicitors, being frequently involved in transferring the ownership of houses and shares, also use *equity* and *equities* in the senses discussed above. Solicitors (and barristers) have a much older meaning for *equity* in a notion or system of justice that is applied concurrently with common or statute law. The underlying sense, however—that of what is due or fair—is the same. Hence we may now note how a common strand of meaning has allowed *equity* to extend into several different but related fields. Despite its spread, the word remains a technical one: as one building society assistant manager confessed, 'I've used it over the phone to customers without thinking, and had to sort myself out'.

ERM
See **Exchange Rate Mechanism**

error
In banking, building societies and life assurance, used in its everyday sense of 'mistake'. A letter telling a customer that an account is overdrawn may end with a sentence such as 'We are advising you so that any error on our part or yours may be

corrected'. Backstage, however, *error* is little used, **difference** being the preferred word.

escalate

In life assurance, to increase pension payments at regular intervals. The term is very much restricted to shop talk; *increase* is the simple equivalent term used in the literature for most prospective customers.

See also **dynamize**

ESTO

In building societies, the acronym for **either signature to operate**. It indicates that, where an account is held in two names, the account holders have authorized the society to accept the signature of either of them on withdrawals, etc. Within a branch, the acronym is frequently used as a verb, so that one may (over)hear, 'Don't forget to get them to ESTO /'ɛstoʊ/ it' or 'Has that new account been ESTO'd /'ɛstoʊd/?'

See also **ASR**

Exchange Rate Mechanism

A device of the European Monetary System which attempts to remove the wilder swings in exchange rates among most currencies of the European Community. An exchange rate is calculated, and each currency's rate is allowed to vary from this only within tight constraints. When Britain finally appplied for entry to the mechanism, in October 1990, the rate for sterling was set at Deutschmarks 2.95 with six per cent margins, giving permitted extremes of DM 2.78 and DM 3.13.

F

fall due

See **mature**

favour

In banking, building societies and life assurance, a term once in widespread use, but obsolete by the mid-twentieth century, to refer to a customer's letter. Guides to commercial correspondence written in the early 1900s frowned upon *letter* alone as being too brusque. Either it was premodified ('Your esteemed letter . . .'), or *favour* was substituted ('We are in receipt of your favour . . .'), or the two were brought together ('Your esteemed favour . . .'). The term does live on, in a different sense, in the phrase *in favour of*, which in the context of cheques means 'payable to': 'Please make your cheque in favour of XYZ plc'.

fifties

In banking and building societies in the UK, 50 pence coins or £50 notes; in the USA, $50 bills.

See Appendix 2 for a discussion of the functions of financial terminology.

FIMBRA

See **Financial Intermediaries, Managers & Brokers Regulatory Association**

Financial Intermediaries, Managers & Brokers Regulatory Association (FIMBRA)

One of the five **self-regulating organizations** in the UK assisting the **Securities and Investment Board** in providing some measure of protection to investors, as authorized by the Secretary of State for Trade and Industry under the Financial Services Act of 1986.

See also **brokerage**

financial planning questionnaire

In banking, building societies and life assurance, a form completed by a financial adviser to fulfil the requirement placed on members of the professions to 'know the customer' before offering **best advice**.

financial services adviser

See **cashier**

fives

In banking and building societies in the UK, 5 pence coins or £5 notes; in the USA, $5 bills.

See Appendix 2 for a discussion of the functions of financial terminology.

flat rate

In banking, building societies and life assurance, a rate of interest normally quoted first in relation to **loans**. If one were to borrow £100 at 10 per cent on 1 January, promise to repay it after one year, and do just that, ie turn up on 1 January of the following year with £110 capital and interest, then the rate would indeed be as quoted as 10 per cent. In practice, this very rarely happens. Instead, a borrower is expected to make repayments, probably monthly, during the course of the year. Consequently, the debt steadily decreases, giving a *true rate* that is far higher than this flat rate (normally around double). To avoid giving the wrong impression, lenders are obliged to quote an **annual percentage rate of charge(APR)** which takes not only the true rate but also any other charges into account.

float

In building societies, cash held by a **cashier** at the start of the business day. In common with many commercial undertakings, notably shops, a building society begins each day with a cash float. In shops, the purpose of the float is to enable change to be given to early customers. During the day, a shop cashier will amass notes and coin as takings, and will pay these in at suitable intervals to a central office, perhaps, or a bank, leaving just a float from which to give change. In building societies, the float is the cash held to pay withdrawals, again to early customers, before cash has been paid in by depositors, and thus effectively equates with the banker's secondary use of **till**.

fluctuating balance

In banking, in theory, any *balance* which changes in an irregular fashion. To a banker, however, it has the rather more specific sense of 'frequently shifting between credit and debit'. Thus, if the balance on your **current account** is **overdrawn** to varying degrees for a few days each month before your salary arrives, you may receive a letter from your bank manager referring to this fluctuating balance, possibly as a prelude to offering you systematic overdraft facilities (see **limit**).

fly-balance

In banking, to **balance** at the first attempt. This successful attempt is alternatively known (amongst other things) as a *shotter*. Eric Partridge's *Dictionary of Slang and Unconventional English* suggests that *shotter* derives from 'at the first shot'. Although no etymology is suggested for *fly-balance*, Partridge does list *fly* as 'have a fly (at it), to try it; to make an attempt'. It is possible, therefore, that *fly-balance* and *shotter* have similar origins, in that each refers to an attempt (at balancing figures) and hence to one that is immediately successful. However, we should note that another term in use in this sense is *flyer*—the particular cry of joy being 'A flyer to a penny!' Now, as the *Oxford English Dictionary* records, *flyer* is used in many contexts for 'one who or that which moves with exceptional speed', and such a definition is clearly pertinent to a balance achieved immediately rather than after laborious checking.

In the north-east of England some branches use *plumpo*, and if one has the good fortune to get a plumpo, one has *plumped*. This would seem to be a borrowing of the dialect use of *plump*, recorded in Wright's *English Dialect Dictionary* with various meanings, such as 'plump out: straight out, without equivocation', 'plump and plain: straight out, without ceremony'— exactly the way bankers like their books to balance.

flyer

See **fly balance**

Footsie

A pseudo-acronym used popularly for the **Financial Times-Stock Exchange 100 Share Index (FT-SE)**. Generally speaking, the index reflects the overall change in value of the shares of the top 100 companies in the UK that are listed on the Exchange, although there are some exceptions. The index was introduced in January 1984 with a base of 1000, and is recalculated literally every 60 seconds of the trading day.

foreign bill

In banking, any **bill** that is not drawn and payable within the British Isles, or on some resident of the British Isles. **Foreign bill** must be one of the most misleading terms a newcomer to banking could meet. It is not a bill in the layperson's normal sense of the word—an account rendered for payment—but a bill of exchange; neither is it drawn in a foreign currency, but in sterling. Foreign bills may be dealt with in a variety of ways, but the most common concerns British exporters of goods. To obtain payment, the exporter **draws** a bill on the importer; the exporter's bank in Britain sends the bill to an agent (another bank), usually in the importer's own town, which obtains payment of the bill from the importer and transmits the **proceeds** back to Britain.

Because this may be a lengthy process, such bills are often drawn payable, for example, *thirty days after date* or *thirty days after sight hereof*. Under the entry for *bill* is noted the fact that a cheque is merely 'a bill of exchange drawn on a banker payable on demand'. Here we have the basic form of a bill, drawn on a person other than a banker, and not necessarily payable immediately it is received by the **drawee**.

foreign clerk

In banking, a clerk whose duties include buying and selling foreign currencies, handling **foreign bills**, etc. The potential ambiguity residing in the written form is resolved in speech in the way that English normally handles such problems. Where it is a particular type that is indicated—in this case, a clerk with specified duties—then it is the first word in the pair which carries the primary stress: /'fɒrın klɑːk/ . Were the two words to be given equal stress— /'fɒrın 'klɑːk/— then a clerk with unspecified duties, but who came from abroad, would be indicated. Where English decides to form a hyphenated or compound noun from such pairs, it is always the type where the first word carries the predominant stress that is changed, eg /'blæk 'bɛri/ becoming /'blækbəri/. Foreign clerk, in banking usage, is thus a prime candidate for hyphenating/compounding.

fortress counter or fortress till

In banking and building societies, a till which is supplied with bullet-proof glass and/or other measures to protect the **cashiers**. It contrasts with one which is **open plan**.

FPQ

See **financial planning questionnaire**

free standing additional voluntary contributions (FSAVCs)

In banking, building societies and life assurance, contributions made by people who wish to increase their pensions, made into a scheme of their own choice. They thus contrast with **additional voluntary contributions**, which are directed to a pension scheme of which one is already a member.

front end loading

1 In life assurance, increasing **assurance** premiums to produce investment **funds**. The **premium** for an endowment, with-profits assurance policy can be split into three components: (a) a charge for cover, (b) the investment portion, which produces the lump sum together with **bonuses** at the end of the period, and (c) expenses, such as commission, the cost of producing the policy, charges for handling renewals, and the like. Some companies, to show large bonuses as a selling feature, add an amount to that required under (b), which makes the premiums slightly more expensive but the return higher. It is this augmentation process which is referred to in the trade as *front end loading*.

2 Also in life assurance, taking administrative charges from premiums paid in the early years only of a life assurance policy. Where a policy is taken out principally as an investment vehicle, as the term of the policy progresses, such an arrangement enables less of the premium to be used in this way, with a corresponding increase in the part actually invested. Here, therefore, it is element (c)—the expenses—which we find loaded at the front end.

Front end loading, then, which might sound as though it had been culled from the language of road hauliers, turns out to be one of those phrases that mean different things to different people within the same profession.

FSAVCs
See **free standing additional voluntary contributions**

FT-SE
See **Footsie**

full set off
See **set off**

fund
In life assurance, a general pool of money created by premiums; or a particular pool, such as a pension fund. In both these uses, the central meaning is of a stock of money created to enable payments to be made for specified purposes. When used as a verb, it means maintaining a fund at a viable level. For instance, if a fund is established to provide pensions of two-thirds of final salary for employees of a named firm, the fund has to be looked at regularly to ensure that the rate of input is adequate to cover future outgoings (that rate being known as the *funding rate*). In other words, care has to be taken to ensure that the fund is adequately funded. If this turns out not to be the case, it may be necessary to make injections to the fund from other sources.

The term is very much one 'for internal use only'. Whilst within the office a life assurance manager might say to a colleague that certain self-employed customers wanted to 'fund for their retirement', in conversation with the customers concerned that same manager is likely to switch to, for example, 'make provision for your retirement'.

See also **funds** and **mortgage funds**

funding rate
See **fund**

funds

In banking and building societies, 'money' in all its forms, as in 'I should be obliged if you would advise me when funds will be available to repay the debt.'

There would seem to be a reluctance on the part of the financial institutions to mention by name their principal commodity—money. The reasons for this shunning of the ordinary word are varied. Whilst economists may find it useful to define *money* as broadly 'anything that is generally acceptable as a means of exchange' (G Crowther, *An Outline of Money*, 1948), banking and building society staff are wise to concede that, to the members of the public with whom they deal, money probably has the restricted sense of 'notes and coin'. A vaguer, more encompassing term such as *funds* is therefore useful to suggest (in addition to cash) cheques, bills of exchange, postal orders, etc. Secondly, *funds* appears to have reached the status of a one-word cliché. Every repeated use helps to ensure its perpetuation. Thirdly, there is a likelihood that *money* is excluded on the grounds of its very ordinariness: such a commonplace word would not convey the seriousness of the situations in which *funds* is preferred. Intermingled with, and thereby interlinking, these points is the word's social function. Despite the avowed intentions of removing barriers between the institutions and their customers, a word drawn from the technical vocabulary reinforces the image of special knowledge and expertise: everyone uses *money*, but only financiers handle *funds*.

See Appendix 2 for a fuller discussion of the functions of financial terminology.

G

general clearing
In banking, cheques accepted by a branch of a **collecting bank**, drawn on branches of other **clearing banks**, and grouped together for transmission through the **clearing**. It is thus distinguished from **branch clearing**, which comprises cheques drawn on other branches of the same bank.

green, green book, grey book
See **colour terms**

grey list
See **black list**

gross rate
In banking and building societies, an interest rate quoted without deduction of income tax. As one building society official commented, 'We use *net* and *gross rates* a tremendous amount, but it's amazing how many people it doesn't mean anything to.' Building societies have long had the problem, acquired a few years ago by the banks, of explaining their interest rates to investors because, unlike some other institutions, they have been liable for the income tax on the interest paid to those investors. (This is no longer wholly the case with the abolition of **composite rate tax** in the UK with effect from 6 April 1991. Whether the terminological confusion will increase or decrease as a result remains to be seen.)

Whereas a government bond may advertise a single, gross rate (ie without any deduction of tax) of 12 per cent, a bank or building society will often quote two rates. The first of these is the net rate: if this is 9.75 per cent, then £9.75 will be the amount actually added to an account each year for each £100 invested (assuming that the interest is credited only once per year—see **compounded annual rate** for the situation where this is not the case). If the banks and building societies are not to lose all their investors, it is necessary for them to explain their apparently low rate of interest in comparison to the 12 per cent quoted above. This is done by reference to the second, gross rate, in this case 13 per cent, which indicates what rate of interest would have had to be paid to leave the investor with 9.75 per cent after the deduction of basic income tax.

These calculations are probably easier to understand if they are presented in reverse order. Basic rate tax is taken here as 25 per cent; 25 per cent of 13 is 3.25; 13 minus 3.25 is 9.75.

H

half

In banking, along with the more common plural **halves**, the now obsolete ten-shilling notes. These terms are strongly remembered from the author's own early days spent in banking as in-house words where the function of promoting social cohesion among the staff was probably stronger than the merely representational. In particular, to ask for a withdrawal from one's account in *new halves*, ie mint condition ten-shilling notes, was to give an unmistakable sign that one was a member of staff. The phrase could be used quite deliberately in a branch many miles from home as a shibboleth, in the certain knowledge that the user would be instantly welcomed as a fellow banker.

The term is now of historical interest, as it did not survive the process of decimalization in 1971. A pocketful of oddly-shaped coins was by no means as attractive as a walletful of crisp new notes and, in any case, inflation soon made the 50 pence piece too small a unit in which to carry the bulk of one's cash.

hard copy

In banking and building societies, a permanent copy of all responses to enquiries on customers' accounts made during a day by computer terminal. Responses of this kind are of an essentially ephemeral nature—the information is for immediate use, but is subsequently of little interest. Nevertheless, just as **waste** sheets in banking are, in fact, retained for several years, so a computer terminal also produces a duplicate, permanent record of all the data it provides. This record is known as the *hard copy*, a term which, with the spread of computerization, is now in wide use.

hit rate

In building societies, a figure indicating the degree of success enjoyed by staff in encouraging the opening of new accounts. The building societies' forceful marketing policies have added directly to in-house vocabularies, and *hit rate* is an egregious example. New customers are the lifeblood of the building society movement, and attracting them is no longer the 'hit and miss' affair it may once have been. To discover, objectively, how successful not only particular branches but individual **cashiers** are in this respect, at least one society calculates how many new accounts are opened by each cashier per total number of transactions handled by that cashier. Instead of expressing the result as a percentage, the fraction is inverted, ie the number of transactions is divided by the number of new accounts, and the dividend is the *hit rate*. Algebraically, the formula is $H = T/N$, where $H = $ hit rate, $T = $ number of transactions, and $N = $ number of new accounts opened. The following hypothetical example, involving three cashiers who each handle 100 transactions in a given period, illustrates the process:

Cashier A	Cashier B	Cashier C
100	100	100
5	8	10
Hit rate = 20	Hit rate = 12.5	Hit rate = 10

Because the computation involves an inverted fraction, the best performance, that of Cashier C, is indicated by the lowest rate. A term which may strike one as being unduly fierce (cf *hit man*) to be used by such socially responsible organizations is, in fact, an accurate indicator of the aggression involved.

The phrase appears to be gaining ground in quite different spheres. *The Times* of 4 August 1990 carried the following item:

The Serious Fraud Office has been criticized for taking too long to bring cases to court. There is also a feeling, which Mr Wood thinks is unjustified, that the team's 'hit-rate' is not high enough. He says that most big fraud cases are by definition difficult to investigate and that his officials should not expect to win every case.

home service

In life assurance, the provision of both **assurance** and **insurance** via **agents** of the companies who call at policyholders' homes. It thus encompasses the earlier notion of **industrial assurance**.

honour

In banking, to pay (a cheque). In a letter to a recalcitrant customer, the use of the unglossed technical term *honour* in 'It will not be possible to honour future cheques' is a particularly strong factor in maintaining an air of formality which is in keeping with the seriousness (at least to the banker) of the matter. It helps to create the social distance between banker and customer which may make it easier for the former to handle an uncomfortable situation.

hot money

In building societies, money invested with a society for too short a time to allow the society to make use of it. *Hot money* is as much a part of the argot of financiers as it is that of thieves, although the connotations for each fraternity are happily rather different. The savings of several people are required to provide the funds for a single mortgage loan, and building societies are therefore keen to attract deposits from any legitimate source. Many professionals—principally solicitors and accountants—put money with building societies on behalf of their clients (and, in reciprocation, may have new clients directed to them by the societies). Some, however, are notorious for depositing funds one week and withdrawing them the next in order to replace them elsewhere for a better financial return. Such money is worse than useless to the societies, who pay interest on it from the day it is received, incur administration costs in its handling, but then find that it has disappeared before they have been able to utilize it. It is this money, which has such a quick turnover that the societies would prefer never to have it in the first place, that is derogatorily labelled *hot* in some societies. (Others employ the more formal *short term money*.)

The phrase is in use in international as well as domestic deposit-taking institutions. The following comment appeared in the main story carried by *The Times* on 15 September 1980:

It is felt that a large cut in interest rates would persuade some of the hot money attracted to London in recent months to move on, thereby pushing the pound's parity down.

house

In banking, as in some other contexts, a commercial company. This is an old-established word: the *Oxford English Dictionary* cites 'Treasurer of the house of the Indias' from 1582. *Counting-house* precedes this by more than a century: *Cowntinge hows* was in use around 1440 to indicate a building or room devoted to bookkeeping and commercial correspondence. By the seventeenth century, *counting-house* was already being superseded by *office*, but *house* continues in several financial contexts.

According to Eric Partridge's *Dictionary of Slang and Unconventional English, the House* (ie with initial capital and preceded by the definite article) came into colloquial use among **brokers** around 1810 to mean the Stock Exchange, thereby apparently predating the use of the same term to refer to the House of Commons by more than ten years. Whilst both these usages remain extant, the latter is widely understood (parliamentary reporting in the mass media being influential here), but the former is restricted to members of the stock-market fraternity.

Bankers do not often use the word *house* as a free-standing noun. Instead it is generally used attributively, being most frequently linked with *debit*. A *house bill* is defined as 'a bill of exchange drawn by a business house on itself' (*OED*), and it would therefore be easy to fall into the trap of assuming that a *house debit* is the same thing under a slightly different name. In fact, *house debit* is the term used by bankers to refer to any cheque that is drawn on their own particular branch. It most frequently occurs when customers of a branch pay in, for the credit of their accounts, cheques drawn by other customers of the same branch. Those cheques would become part of the house debits section of a **batch**. That section is itself occasionally referred to by the shortened form *house*, so that a newcomer to the **remittances** department of a branch may be told, 'We put our own cheques under *house*.' However, see **batch** for the possible disappearance of this system.

When banks do **draw** their own variety of *house bills*, these latter are not known by that name at all, but as *drafts on head office*, *drafts on branches*, or *branch cheques*, and collectively as **bankers' drafts**.

house bill
See **house**

house credit
In banking, a paying-in slip received over the counter of a branch where the account concerned is maintained at that branch.

See also *house debit* under **house**

house debit
See **house**

I

ID

/aɪˈdiː/ In banking and building societies, a means of proving one's identity. The abbreviation is derived from the first two letters of *identification*, and would seem to be a loan from the civil and military forces, who refer to their identity cards as *ID cards*. Should one find oneself away from home and wishing to cash a cheque without the benefit of either a cheque card or a **credit open**, one is likely to be asked to produce some form of ID. Although the term is in increasingly widespread use, bank and building society personnel report that it still produces puzzled expressions on some faces.

IMRO

See **Investment Management Regulatory Organization**

in-clearing

See **clearing**

in credit clearing

In banking, **credits**, received by a branch, which have been paid in at another bank or branch for transmission via the credit **clearing**; also, the system for handling such credits.

indent

In building societies, an **open cheque** drawn on a local bank in order to maintain cash levels within a branch. Whilst the majority of mortgage repayments over the counter are made by cheque, withdrawals from savings are generally requested in cash. Consequently, although a building society branch's accounts at the end of a day may show a 'surplus' (see **net receipts**), its cash stock may have been depleted. To replenish this, the branch will have an arrangement with a local bank to encash an open cheque. Such a cheque borrows the name used for a paper which requisitions supplies in many industries—an *indent*.

independent financial adviser

In banking, building societies and life assurance, a person who gives impartial counselling (see **best advice**), based on an understanding of the customer's needs and of what is available from a wide range of financial **products**, not just those of one company. The notion of **polarization** demands that those authorized to give investment advice must fall clearly into one of two categories—either an **agent** (or **representative**) or an independent financial adviser.

indorse

See **endorse**

industrial life assurance

In life assurance, an approach introduced in the mid-nineteenth century as an alternative to **ordinary life assurance**. Life assurance companies' services were initially utilized by only a small proportion of the population. Various methods of attempting to broaden this market were tried after 1850, such as the introduction of group schemes, and the increase in the number of agencies and branches. However, given the fact that ordinary life assurance was paid for through relatively large premiums at relatively long intervals— annually or quarterly—it is clear to see (with the benefit of hindsight) that such moves were essentially doomed until working people enjoyed a large increase in affluence, and this took another century to arrive.

What happened instead was the introduction of industrial life assurance. This enabled premiums, often of only one penny a week, to be paid towards policies which normally gave cover of £10 or less; it revolutionized the life assurance market. However, the number of industrial assurances taken up per year (from all industrial life assurance offices) has fallen from 4.9 million in 1949, through 3.3 million in 1975 to under 2.9 million in 1987. Whilst the introduction of industrial policies, then, gave a great impetus to the life assurance movement as a whole, their importance is now steadily declining.

See also **home service**

in order

1 In banking, applied to a cheque having no *technical irregularities*. These irregularities concern the points at which errors may occur in the writing of a cheque—the date, concurrence of amounts in words and figures, etc. When the matter arises of returning a cheque unpaid because there are not enough **funds** in the customer's account to cover it, a manager will normally scrutinize it very carefully to ensure that it is technically in order. If it is not, most managers will prefer to return it for that reason, (eg that it is *out of date*), rather than the potentially damaging *Refer to Drawer* (see **answer**). Human nature being the way it is, of course, some customers who are temporarily financially embarrassed play this system to their advantage by making deliberate mistakes when writing out their cheques.

2 Also in banking, applied to an account having either a **credit** balance, or a **debit** balance not exceeding a **limit** set by the bank.

In the case of both cheque and account, the opposite is *out of order*.

inspector

1 In banking, an official who visits branches, either routinely to ensure that all procedures are being properly adhered to, or specially in cases of suspected fraud (see also **ticker**).

2 In life assurance, a life **assurance** salesperson. Whilst all the major **fund**-gathering institutions now adopt marketing policies of varying degrees of aggressiveness, it is only the life assurance companies who refer to their front-line troops as *salesmen*. However, there is a growing preference for the euphemistic, non-sexist but (some might say) self-aggrandizing appellation, *inspectors*.

insurable interest

See **write**

insurance

Generally, cover provided against an event that may possibly happen.

See **assurance**

in the red

In banking, as in everyday speech, an expression dating from the days when overdrawn balances were entered in ledgers and statements in red ink. The phrase was never greatly favoured by bankers, who are not concerned so much with whether an account is in **debit** or **credit** as with whether it is **in order** or not. Whilst a customer with a debit balance of £190 might describe the account as being *in the red*, if the branch manager had placed a **limit** of £200 on the account (ie agreed that the customer could overdraw to that extent), that account would be *in order*.

Amongst the new generation of bank clerks who have known only computerized accounts, printed wholly in black, the term is virtually obsolete.

Investment Management Regulatory Organization (IMRO)

One of the five **self-regulating organizations** in the UK assisting the **Securities and Investment Board** in providing some measure of protection to investors, as authorized by the Secretary of State for Trade and Industry under the Financial Services Act of 1986.

J

joint account mandate

See **mandate**

K

k out

In building societies, to remove an erroneous entry from a ledger. At least one building society has enriched its word-store by this borrowing from the field of computers (the *K* key on the keyboard being the one to depress to put matters right). The process of removing the offending item can be put in train by annotating it with the code letter *K* on the appropriate sheet. All that needs to be said to indicate that this type of correction needs to be made is 'We'll have to K /keɪ/ that item out.'

See also **mispost**

keyman assurance

In life assurance, cover provided for the benefit of a business on the life of a member of its staff whose existence is crucial to that business. Although this cover is, of course, available regardless of the gender of the person concerned, the continued use of the title *keyman* in these supposedly less sexist days comes as something of a surprise, particularly given the replacement of life assurance *salesmen* by **inspectors**.

See also **term assurance** and **write**

L

last survivor policy

In life assurance, a policy providing life **assurance** cover for both husband and wife, but paying out only when both partners have died, and thus avoiding tax complications after the first death.

LAUTRO

See **Life Assurance & Unit Trust Regulatory Organization**

legal tender

The money that a creditor is legally obliged to accept when offered in payment. At the time of writing, the limits on small change as legal tender in the UK are as follows:

Coins	Maximum Value
1p and 2p	20p
5p and 10p	£5
20p and 50p	£10
£1	unlimited

liabilities

See **equity**

life

See **life assured**

Life Assurance & Unit Trust Regulatory Organization (LAUTRO)

One of the five **self-regulating organizations** in the UK assisting the **Securities and Investment Board** in providing some measure of protection to investors, as authorized by the Secretary of State for Trade and Industry under the Financial Services Act of 1986.

See also **assurance, unit trust**

life assured

In life assurance, the person on whose life an **assurance** policy is effected. *Life*, therefore, is not used here in the abstract sense of 'animate existence', but has become a quite tangible person. Hence, it is common practice for company forms to ask for *the name of the life assured*, and for *evidence of the life assured's good health*, and even to refer to *the death of the life assured*.

It is important to remember here that *the life (assured)* and *the assured* are not necessarily one and the same person. If a woman takes out a policy on the life of her husband, it is his life which is *assured*, whilst she becomes *the assured*. Close consideration of what is involved in the use of the word *life* in this context leads one to the conclusion that, although the companies' intentions are doubtless of the very best in avoiding reference to unpleasant certainties, the word has been twisted from its original meaning in a truly Orwellian fashion. The real concern of a *life* policy, of course, is the *death* of the person named. Linguistic contortion reaches its limits in the term *whole life policy*, which is one where the proceeds are payable only on death.

If death is a modern taboo, then personal finance closely approaches it in the way in which we hide details of it from our neighbours. Euphemisms are consequently in evidence in this area too. A policy that provides cover for the smallest possible charge is known as an *economy plan* or *low cost plan* policy. It must be stressed that it would be illegitimate to criticize the companies for their role in this. We (the public) have only ourselves to blame if we find *economy plan whole life policy* sweeter to our ears than *cheap death policy*.

Life Offices Association

See **office**

limit

In banking, the extent to which a bank agrees that an account may be overdrawn. Thus, a branch manager may write to a customer to confirm that 'a limit of £500 has been placed on your account'.

list

In banking and building societies, to enter sums in an adding machine so that they are produced on a list and totalled.

See also **cast**

loaded premium

In life assurance, a **premium** which is higher than the norm, because the company regards the customer as presenting a higher risk. This may be because of a poor health record, or for a number of other reasons, such as participation in hazardous sports (e.g. parachuting or hang-gliding).

loan

In banking and building societies, in its ordinary sense, an amount lent. Banks tend to make a careful distinction between a *loan* and an **overdraft**. Whilst the latter is granted on a *current account*, where the balance frequently changes and the interest chargeable with it, a loan is normally made available on a quite separate account. This is administratively neater for both parties, allowing fixed, regular repayments and the possibility of calculating the interest charge in advance (assuming no change in the rate).

lock out

In banking, building societies and life assurance, to render a branch unable to obtain information from a computer terminal because of electrical or mechanical breakdown. Thus, for **cashiers** who are warm and dry inside their branch premises, there is no contradiction in saying to a customer who has requested a balance, 'I'm afraid we're locked out again.' In this context it is a synonym of *down*, and like many such computer-based terms is now in widespread use.

long dog

In banking, a long, narrow slip of paper on which a **cashier** may list about 20 **debit** items. It is so called by humorous analogy of its shape to that of a dachshund.

See also **meat ticket**

low cost plan

See **life assured**

lump sum

In life assurance, a single, relatively large payment. Customers may encounter the term as payers (see **annuity**) or as recipients. Many pension schemes provide for a lump sum on retirement of, say, 1.5 times final annual salary, to be followed by regular monthly payments which are, of course, much smaller.

M

machine, machine room
See **machinist**

machinist
In banking, one who operated earlier accounting machines, now the user of a computer with similar functions. Despite the fact that the updating of information on customers' accounts is now accomplished via computer links, **terminal operator** has yet to come into universal usage between clerks, the older-established *machinist* being still preferred by many, eg 'Jane's going on a machinist's course next week.' Perhaps even more telling is the fact that in establishments where those machines have long since disappeared and the rooms that housed them have been taken over for quite different purposes (eg rest and recreation areas), it is still quite common for such a room to retain the nostalgic title *machine room.*

Machine and *machinist* themselves, in the context of mechanized recording of bookkeeping transactions, date back only as far as the late 1950s, prior to which all accounts had been entered by hand. In the early 1970s, at the end of the author's own banking career, **deposit accounts** were still being **posted** manually.

mail transfer (MT)
In banking, a method of transferring sums of money abroad, between banks, using the postal services.

See also **telegraphic transfer**

mandate
1 In banking, a form indicating that one customer may act on behalf of more than one, and authorizing a bank to accept instructions accordingly. The most common example is the *Joint Account Mandate* which is taken from a husband and wife opening an account together; this form allows the bank to

accept the signature of either one of them on cheques drawn against the account. *Partnership Mandates* and *Company Mandates* fulfil similar purposes. Compare the use of phrases such as 'a mandate from the people/members' in political and trade union circles.

2 Also in banking, to instruct an employer, a company in which one holds shares, and the like, to pay salary, dividends, etc direct to one's bank account. In the case of dividend payments, the document giving the instruction is known as a *dividend mandate*.

3 In building societies, originally an instruction to make regular payments between accounts held by the society. In this context, *mandate* is thus the equivalent of the banker's internal **standing order**. In at least one society, the term has extended its area of meaning to include transactions made in compliance with such instructions, a particular sum so transferred being itself referred to simply as a *mandate*.

mark

In banking, to write a reason on a cheque for returning it unpaid. Thus, one might receive a standard letter from one's bank, referring to a cheque that one had paid in a few days earlier, stating that the cheque 'has been returned unpaid by the Bank on which it is drawn marked *Out of Date*'. 'With the answer' is often used as a synonymous phrase for *marked* (see also **answer**).

mature

In banking and life assurance, to become due for payment (said of various financial documents). Just as a *life* may *die* (see **life assured**), so an inanimate policy is said to *mature* and to have a *maturity value*. There are close links here with banking and general commercial parlance. **Bills** of exchange, excluding cheques, are usually **drawn** to *fall due*—become payable—at some future date. When this date arrives, the bill is said to have *matured*, a term shown by the *Oxford English Dictionary* to have been in use since at least 1861. There are parallel tendencies in the financial press reports of Stock Exchange dealings, where shares may 'lose ground' or 'leap ahead'.

meat ticket

In banking, a slip of paper on which a **cashier** writes the amount of cash paid in by a customer, together with details of the account to be *credited*. If a credit consists simply of cheques, then there is no difficulty in processing it through the **waste**. If everything is in order, the cheques, as **debits**, will collectively balance against the total of the credit. Where cash is involved, however, a problem arises from the fact that the cash is retained by the cashier, leaving the **waste clerk** with no balancing item for that part (or whole) of the credit. There are various possible solutions to this: that adopted by at least one bank involves the cashier in writing, on a small, rectangular piece of paper, the sum of money and name of the customer (or that of the account-holding branch if the item is not a **house credit**). Possibly because of its shape and size, and the fact that the details inscribed would correspond with the price and description of a cut of meat in a butcher's shop, it is irreverently referred to as a *meat ticket*. Alternatively, it is possible that the term may have been introduced by older members of staff as a loan from the vocabulary of the armed forces, where, for more gruesome reasons, it means an identity disc.

See also **long dog**

meet

In banking, to pay (a cheque or other **bill**). If a cheque is technically **in order**, sufficient funds are available in the account, and there are no special reasons for returning the cheque (such as the death of the **drawer**), then it must be met.

memorandum

In banking, a now obsolete term for a **counterfoil** to a paying-in slip. The *Oxford English Dictionary* records instances of this term, with the specific meaning of 'a record of money owed', dating from the early seventeenth century. Bearing in mind that the bank would have placed the sum shown to the **credit** of the relevant customer's account, it is quite logical that it should have issued a document which, by its title, acknowledged its own position as a debtor.

minimum lending rate (MLR)

In banking and building societies, the rate of interest at which the Bank of England, acting in its capacity as 'lender of last resort', would lend money, on the money market, to the commercial banks. Although it is doubtful if more than a small minority of the population had anything beyond the slightest comprehension of its meaning, the phrase was frequently used by the financial commentators of the mass media, and by the institutions themselves. A standard letter sent out by one major building society in November 1979 began with the unglossed statement 'Minimum Lending Rate has increased to 17 per cent.'

MLR was introduced on 14 October 1972 to replace the old Bank Rate, and reported in *The Times* (and elsewhere, of course) the following day. Despite the necessity of mentioning it on many intervening occasions, it was not until 23 December of that year that *The Times* first referred to it by the abbreviation *MLR*. After that date the use of the abbreviated form steadily increased, and became common on radio and television news broadcasts, at least after the full form had been used once or more in a particular transmission. The abbreviation did not appear to be sufficiently widely known to permit its use in those circumstances without an immediately preceding or succeeding explanation.

MLR was officially suspended on 19 August 1981, so that both the phrase and its abbreviation are probably destined for the history books. However, it is worth adding that, although the Bank of England no longer exercises direct control, having retained the right to reactivate MLR only in exceptional circumstances, its indirect influence is still very strong. In November 1990, for example, when the commercial banks were pressing for a reduction in their **base rates** (supposedly set independently by the banks themselves) to below 14 per cent, the Bank of England forced them to continue paying at that level on their own substantial borrowings, thereby putting any base rate change out of the question. *Plus ça change?*

MIRAS

See **mortgage interest relief at source**

mispost

In banking, building societies and life assurance, to enter a transaction wrongly in an account. The term is widespread in accounting circles generally.

See also **k out** and **post**

MLR

See **minimum lending rate**

mortgage

In banking and building societies, prior to 1926, the conveyance of property, temporarily, to a lender for the period of the loan, as either **direct security** or **collateral security**. The Law of Property Act of 1925 amended the procedure to the effect that, as far as land was concerned, a mortgage ceased to involve a conveyance. In brief, a mortgagee of land now enjoys the rights of someone holding a long lease (normally 3000 years), although the arrangement is, of course, automatically ended on repayment of the loan. Alternatively, under Section 87 of the same Act, a mortgage can be created through execution of a deed indicating that a **charge** on the land has been taken. This is both more common and easier for customers to understand, whilst affording lenders the same rights.

In common with all other relational opposites in English which end in *-or* and *-ee*, the provider takes the first suffix (*mortgagor*) and the recipient the second (*mortgagee*). The customer is mortgaging the property in return for the loan, whilst the institution is taking what one hopes is a temporary financial interest in it. However, use of the terms by customers is not consistently in line with this, as *mortgage* has extended its meaning to cover the loan itself. It is certainly common for people to say, 'I'm going to the building society to get a mortgage.'

This suggestion—that it is the institution which gives rather than receives the mortgage—is not resisted in the literature issued by the lenders. At the time of writing, leaflets carry the following 'wealth warning': 'Your home is at risk if you do not keep up repayments on a mortgage or other loan secured on it', where *mortgage or other loan* seemingly takes the side of those who see a mortgage as being identical with a loan (although it is possible that there is a deliberately produced ellipsis to avoid the clumsy *mortgage loan or other loan*). Similarly, an estate agent was quoted in *The Times* of 30 July 1990 as saying, 'the first-time buyer vanished at the end of February and has hardly been seen since. There will be no meaningful return until interest rates fall a minimum of 1 per cent and the mortgagee is confident there will be no further increase for at least 12 months', where it is virtually certain that *mortgagee* indicates the borrower and not the lender.

Legal precision notwithstanding, it now appears to be the case that most of the people involved—lenders, borrowers, and at least some intermediaries—think of the institutions as being the mortgagors and their customers as the mortgagees.

See also **endowment mortgage** and **repayment mortgage**

mortgagee, mortgagor
See **mortgage**

mortgage funds
In banking and building societies, money available to an institution to lend to mortgagors (see **mortgage**, **funds**).

Mortgage Interest Relief At Source (MIRAS)
In banking and building societies, a system introduced with effect from 1 April 1983 whereby the basic income tax relief on the interest paid on a **mortgage** loan is deducted from the borrower's regular repayment. The lending institution reclaims the relief direct from the Inland Revenue.

The net effect is the same as the old system under which the total amount was repaid to the bank or building society with relief being given in the following tax year via the tax coding system, but the newer device has the additional benefit of passing on changes, such as those of rates of tax and interest, very quickly. Whether this golden effect for borrowers (in good times at least) led the coiners of the acronym *MIRAS* /'maɪrəs/ to opt for a near soundalike for the legendary King Midas is unknown.

mortgage protection policy
See **term assurance**

MT
See **mail transfer**

mutilated cheque
See **answer**

N

NBI
See **no book item**

net rate
In banking and building societies, the rate of interest actually applied to investors' accounts, quoted free of income tax at basic rate.

See also **gross rate** and **compounded annual rate**

net receipts
In building societies, the excess of money paid into a society over that paid out; alternatively known as *surplus*. Net receipts are the important ones. If £20 000 is paid in during the course of a day, and £19 999 is paid out, the branch's net receipts amount to only £1.

See also **quota**

no book item (NBI)
In building societies, a transaction carried out without being entered in the customer's **passbook**. For example, a cheque may be paid in for the **credit** of an account without the book being presented. The book is then updated from the branch's internal records the next time the customer takes it in.

non-brokerage, non-commission
See **brokerage**

not negotiable
See **crossing**

not proceeded with (NPW)
In life assurance, applied to an enquiry for a policy by a

prospective customer which goes so far through the process but where finally the enquirer decides against it.

See also **not taken up**

not taken up (NTU)
In life assurance, an enquiry for a policy by a prospective customer which does not get beyond the stage of the company giving the enquirer a quotation of likely benefits, premiums, etc. It should be compared with **not proceeded with**, which also relates to abortive enquiries, where the enquiry went a little further through the system.

NTU
See **not taken up**

NPW
See **not proceeded with**

node site
In banking and building societies, a regionalized computer point, into which branches feed, and from which they receive, data.

O

office

In life assurance, especially when preceded by the word *life*, a synonym for *assurance company*. In assurance/insurance terminology, an office is not necessarily a geographically situated place of business. One of the principal 'trade organizations' is known as the *Life Offices Association*. The *Oxford English Dictionary* traces *Insuring-Office*, with the sense of the company rather than its place of business, to 1646, while the title *The Phoenix Fire Office* was in use in 1782.

ones

In banking and building societies in the UK, 1 penny or £1 coins.

See Appendix 2 for a discussion of the functions of financial terminology.

open cheque

In banking, a cheque which is not **crossed** and which is therefore exchangeable for cash over a bank counter.

opening (a cheque)

See **crossing**

open plan

In banking and building societies, as in general commercial use, an office that has few or no dividing walls or partitions. More specifically, it is sometimes used to refer to counters which have no grilles, bullet-proof glass, or the like (compare **fortress counter**).

ordinary life assurance

In life assurance, cover for relatively large sums, with premiums paid monthly or at longer intervals, often by **banker's order** or **direct debit**. Since the last war, there has been a narrowing of the income differentials which traditionally existed between manual workers and salaried employees. The increase in disposable income available to the lower socioeconomic groups has created a lucrative market previously untouched by the ordinary life assurance companies. Previously, the major volume of life policies was sold by the industrial offices on a door-to-door basis (compare **industrial life assurance** and **office**). After World War 2, an increasing number were sold by intermediaries, supported by national and local advertising campaigns. Post-war affluence has turned more people towards assurance as a form of investment.

ors

In banking, an abbreviation for **others**. Where holders of a particular account are more than three in number (a situation that crops up fairly often with trustees), the practice is to show (for example, on a cheque destined for the account) only the first trustee's name, and to add *and others* or, more usually, *& Ors*. It is, one may note, the exact commercial equivalent of the academic *et al.*

out clearing

See **clearing**

out credit clearing

In banking, the **credits** received by a branch for transmission via the credit **clearing** to the branches where the beneficiaries' accounts are held; also, the system for handling such credits.

See also **in credit clearing**

out of date

See **answer**

out of order

See **in order**

overdraft

In banking, a situation created by drawing out of one's account more than one has in it. If an overdraft is given prior authorization by the bank, this is normally effected by the manager placing a **limit** on the account, stipulating the extent to which the customer may overdraw. If one attempts to overdraw without such an arrangement, then there is, of course, the risk that one's cheques will be returned unpaid, marked with the **answer** *Refer to Drawer*.

Whilst most customers think of an overdraft as being simply a sort of **loan**, bankers tend to differentiate between the two. An overdraft is granted on a **current account**; consequently, because money will be flowing in and out of the account, the balance will be continually changing, and with it the amount that the bank will be able to charge as interest. A loan, in contrast, will be given on a quite separate account, where the only transactions will be repayments and the application of the interest charged.

overdraw

In banking, to take out of one's **current account** more than one has in it.

See **overdraft**

override

In building societies, a withdrawal made in contravention of the normal rules, but with managerial approval. Thus, a withdrawal on an investment account which created a **debit** balance, or the taking of £500 in cash where the normal limit was £250, would each be referred to as an *override*. The name derives, fairly obviously, from the fact that an official has to override the system to allow it to happen. Overrides are more formally referred to as *overriding withdrawals*.

Compare **overdraft** in banking usage

overriding withdrawal

See **override**

P

paid cheque

In banking, a cheque with the word *paid* stamped on it, the rubber stamp used incorporating a date. This is done in addition to **cancelling** cheques to show that they are **in order**. Some customers request, in addition to their statements, the actual cheques that have been **debited** to their accounts. Banks refer to these as *paid cheques*.

paid up policy

A policy on which no more premiums are to be paid. If you find that your financial circumstances prevent your continuing to pay the **premiums** on your life assurance policy, but if the **surrender value** quoted by the company for cashing in the policy early is not attractive either (and it often isn't), then you could opt instead to have the policy made *paid up*. No more premiums are due, but a proportion of the sum assured would still be payable at the end of the full period.

partnership mandate

See **mandate 1**

passbook

Perhaps obsolescent in banking, but still widely used in building societies, a book in which all transactions are entered, showing the balance each time, to act as a record for the customer. The *Oxford English Dictionary* suggests that it may take its name from the fact that the book passes to and fro between those concerned. The term is probably more current amongst staff than amongst customers, many of whom prefer *bankbook* (especially in the north of England, where *bank* is often used to mean 'building society' anyway).

payee

In banking, the person, etc to whom a cheque is made payable.

See also **favour**

paying bank

In banking, the bank on which a cheque is drawn; for that reason, alternatively known as a *drawee bank*.

Compare **collecting bank**

payment countermanded by order of drawer

See **answer**

PEP

See **personal equity plan**

peripheral mortgage

In banking and building societies, an existing **mortgage** loan when an increase in the loan is being considered. If a current mortgagor (ie borrower) wishes to 'trade up' in the housing market, and requires increased mortgage facilities to do so, the correspondence between the lending institution's branch and its head office may refer to the *peripheral mortgage*. This is a potentially ambiguous term, perhaps suggesting to an outsider the 'mortgage on the limit', ie the extra amount requested. In fact, it is used to denote the 'mortgage within the periphery', ie the amount presently outstanding.

per mille, also per mill or per mil

/pə'mɪl/, occasionally /pə'miːl/ In banking, building societies and life assurance, for each thousand. Modelled, of course, on the much more common *per cent*, this item is the subject of at least one institutional anecdote. During the early 1970s, a new system of charging for a particular foreign exchange service was introduced on the basis of *one per mille*, ie £1 charge for every £1000 involved in the transaction. Unfortunately, the symbol 1‰, being an unfamiliar one, was misread by some staff as 1 per cent, and the story is told that, in branches where this happened, customers were charged ten times the correct amount. Given the natural reluctance of those concerned to identify themselves, the exact degree of truth in all this will probably never be discovered.

personal equity plan (PEP)

In banking, building societies and life assurance, a device introduced in the 1986 UK budget, permitting a tax-efficient way of investing in UK shares. It is normally given the clever acronym *PEP* to suggest injecting a little life into one's investments (cf. **escalate**). A PEP is very much in line with the Conservative philosophy of widening share ownership. In 1990, an individual could invest up to £6000 per year in a PEP and have no liability to income tax (which would otherwise be deducted from dividend payments) and none to capital gains tax when the value of the PEP is realized. The field is now so wide and so complicated, with well over 300 schemes on offer allowing investment in a variety of ways, that specialist guides to the PEPs maze are now available.

The punning acronym is so appealing to marketers of financial services that it has quickly found its way across the Channel to represent a slightly different **product**. The French can now invest in a PEP, too—a *Plan d'Epargne Populaire* ('popular savings plan').

personal identification number (PIN)

In banking and building societies, the number allocated to the holder of a **plastic** card, especially one for use in an **automated teller machine**. Because the number is (supposedly) known only to the customer, it prevents anyone else who may obtain the card from using it. **Cashiers** report, however, that some customers insist on acting against their best interests by revealing their personal identification numbers to other parties.

In writing, the term is normally abbreviated simply to *PIN*. In speech, however, the third element is often oddly duplicated, with both staff and customers talking about *PIN numbers*. This may be accounted for by the fact that *PIN* is pronounced here as an acronym, and that there would be a self-conscious reluctance to say, for example, 'Don't forget you have to put your /pɪn/ in the machine.' However, the tautology has a direct parallel amongst book handlers, where the acronym explanation would not apply: both librarians and assistants in bookshops frequently render *International Standard Book Number* as *ISBN number*.

pick up

In banking, to add previous sub-totals on to new figures. Because, in a large branch, many hundreds of paying-in slips, cheques, etc are handled each day, it is not possible to wait until the close of business to start **balancing** them. They are therefore collected periodically into **batches** by *remittances* (or **waste**) *clerks*. *Picking up* is an important part of the process of handling batches and, as with *batch* itself, the particular way in which *pick up* is used marks it as part of the language of banking. The chief remittances clerk may often be heard reminding the junior members of the team, 'Don't forget to pick up the last batch.'

The term does not refer to the physical handling of a bundle of cheques and credits; instead, it relates to a method of producing running totals for the work that passes through the section during the course of a day. It is necessary for final balancing purposes that a grand total of the figures from all the batches be produced. This can be done by means of a summary sheet, but more often it is effected by adding, on each successive **batch sheet**, the totals from the individual sections from the previous sheet, thereby producing a continually updated aggregate. It is this process of adding interim figures that is known as *picking up*. However, see **batch** concerning the possible disappearance of the whole system.

pick-up

In banking, a previous total to be added to current figures to produce a running total (see **pick up**). If the totals on a **batch sheet** midway through the day look suspiciously small, a clerk may be asked, 'Are you sure you haven't forgotten the pick-ups?'

PIN

See **personal identification number**

pink
See **colour terms**

pipeline

In building societies, **mortgage** applications received but to which agreement has not yet been given. Where an application has simply been physically accepted, there is no legal obligation to proceed, but most building society managers would feel morally bound to be as helpful as possible. Consequently, although the amounts involved do not, at this stage, appear in the branch's lending figures, there is a very real probability that they will do so before long, and these sums are collectively known as the *pipeline*.

If one sees metaphors as being condensed similes, then it is the further stages of the condensation process that are of most interest here. An official at a branch's (regional) head office could telephone and ask, 'What's your pipeline?' rather than, for example, 'How much is in the pipeline?' In other words, *pipeline* has progressed from being a literal container to a figurative one—to the thing 'contained'. The question is asked in a similar form within the office when weekly figures are being prepared ('What's the pipeline?'); or, in this situation, the condensation process can be pushed to its limits with one enquiring simply 'Pipeline?'

place a limit
See **limit**

plastic

In banking and building societies, a generic term for plastic cards issued to customers, encompassing *cashcards* for use in **automated teller machines**, *credit cards*, and others. The free-standing noun is often used in a question to help a customer who has been asked to produce some form of identification (compare **ID**): 'Have you got any (*or* a piece of) plastic on you?'

plastic run

In banking and building societies, a batch of plastic cards (see **plastic**) produced for a number of customers at a time at or via an institution's head office. A branch manager who telephones head office to enquire about a card requested by a customer may well be told, 'Don't worry about it: it's in the next plastic run.'

plump, plumpo
See **fly balance**

polarization
In banking, building societies and life assurance, the process of making a clear-cut distinction between the two types of bodies handling investment business. Such businesses must now be unequivocally either **agents** (or **representatives**), selling for one company only, or **independent financial advisers**, with a heavy emphasis on the word *independent*.

poorly
In banking, a mock-sympathetic term to describe an account whose financial health is giving cause for concern: 'His account's pretty poorly, but I don't think we need to put him on the **black list** yet.'

portfolio selling
In building societies, the encouraging of customers (and potential customers) to make use of as wide a range as possible of a society's services or **products**.

Just how sales-oriented an organization like a present-day building society is may be indicated by this item. As one manager explained:

> We have a range of products, and we are expected to use them all, so if you've got ten things that are available for customers to use and they're only using one of them, there's something wrong with your advice to the customer. We're expected to suggest across the portfolio of products so that the customer can choose them.

The construction 'so that the customers can choose them' rather than '. . . choose from them' may be an unconscious indication of the degree of pressure involved, although there is, of course, no suggestion of a failure to offer **best advice**.

post

In banking, to enter in customers' accounts the house **debits** and **credits** which have come into the branch. The definition which the *Oxford English Dictionary* quotes from 1706 applies exactly today: 'To Post an Account, is to put an Account forward from one Book to another; as to transcribe, or to enter what is written in a Merchant's Waste-Book into the Journal, etc.'

See also **waste**

postdated

See **answer**

premium

In life assurance, the payment (annual, quarterly, monthly, or even weekly) to an insurance/assurance company in return for cover. The word also appears in stock market parlance to refer to the difference between the price at which shares are issued by a company and the higher price at which they are traded on the market. Thus, if XYZ plc is newly formed and asks for 120 pence per share from members of the public, who then discover that the shares are so popular that they can resell them for 150p each, they could be resold at a 30p *premium*. If, unfortunately, the reverse is true and only 90p can be realized, the shares would be traded at a 30p *discount*.

present (for payment)

In banking, to take or send a cheque to the **paying bank** to obtain payment of it; or, if the cheque is returned unpaid, the **answer** indicating the reason.

The phrase is not actually restricted to bankers. Indeed, the spread of its use across the financial institutions is nicely exemplified in the final sentence of a letter received by the customer of a building society a few years ago. Enclosing a cheque in settlement of an insurance claim that had been submitted via the society, the writer asked that the recipient 'present the cheque for payment at the earliest opportunity'. With the best will in the world, there is still the occasional assumption of a general knowledge and understanding of terminology that is in fact quite technical.

See also **collect**

The *Oxford English Dictionary*'s first example of *presenting* in the banking sense dates from only 1900—an indication of the comparatively recent spread of the banking habit: '*Present again* . . . shows that the banker has reason to believe that the cheque will be met.' Since the turn of the century, this particular response (or **answer**) has been amended first to *Please re-present* and then, since the late 1950s, to *Please represent*. As it is bankers themselves who put the cheque back through the *clearing* for a second presentation, there is no loss of clarity in their eyes in the form *represent*. New entrants will almost always hear the word spoken by more senior colleagues before they ever see it in writing, and will therefore, on their first encounter with it on a cheque, interpret it correctly as /riːprɪˈzɛnt/. There must, however, be customers, particularly 'first-generation' ones, who are familiar only with /rɛprɪˈzɛnt/ , and who would wonder what was involved in *representing*.

Corroboration of this claim comes from the long-running saga of northern working-class life, *Coronation Street*. The episode transmitted on 21 January 1981 included an encounter between Fred, a barman in the 'Rover's Return', and Alf, the proprietor of the corner shop. Fred had received a cheque for £150 but, having no bank account of his own, had persuaded Alf to cash it for him and pay it into the shop account. The cheque was subsequently returned unpaid. Alf, not unnaturally, took up the matter with Fred, and the following conversation ensued:

Alf: You see what's stamped there? [*ie on the cheque*]
Fred: Please represent. /rɛprɪˈzɛnt/
Alf: Please represent. /ˈriːprɪzɛnt/ [*with heavy stress on the first syllable*]

priority payment
See **telegraphic transfer**

proceeds
In banking, building societies and life assurance, yet another way of avoiding referring to money—compare **funds**, **remittance**, etc. To be fair, it does have the rather more precise

meaning of 'what is left at the end of a transaction', so that a bank may write to tell you that it has 'credited the proceeds of the sale of the shares to your account', or that your loan will be repaid 'from the proceeds of the life assurance policy'.

There is a satisfying etymological circularity involved here: *proceed* derives from Latin *procedere* ('to advance'), whilst *advance* is one of the institutional synonyms for *loan*.

product

Any service offered by a building society or life assurance company. When building society managers talk of a *portfolio of products*, or life assurance staff refer to *wholesaling our company's products*, they are, of course, being highly metaphorical—these organizations sell services, not artefacts. However, a service is rather a hazy concept, and the idea of selling a service vaguer still. The person unknown in marketing (presumably) who first thought of referring to services as *products* made them, at a stroke, seem far easier to grasp—and consequently to sell.

Correspondence with life assurance companies reveals that there are staff in their head offices bearing designations such as *Products Manager*. There is an insurance organization based in Paris which has the title *Bureau International des Producteurs d'Assurances et des Réassurances*.

proof

See **batch**

proof machine

In banking, a machine on which **batches** are listed to **prove** their accuracy.

proposal

In life assurance, an application from a (prospective) customer for cover, giving relevant personal details. A proposal is similar to an application which forms part of a building society's **pipeline**, in that there is no legal obligation on the company to proceed with it. When the branch office that has taken the proposal form from the would-be client submits it to its head office, the *proposal* becomes a **case**.

prove

1 In banking, to **list** items on a **batch sheet**.

2 In building societies, to balance the books at the end of the day's business.

Q

quota

1 In building societies, the maximum total that a branch is allowed to lend, in any given period, to mortgagors (see **mortgage**). As many customers find this trade term for a lending limit meaningless, *allocation* is often substituted in conversation with the public, although even this latter term may need occasional glossing. The quota is based on the **net receipts** (or *surplus*) for the previous month. It is not difficult to see how quickly in-house language can become incomprehensible to the outsider. Consider how much (or how little) meaning a layperson could extricate unaided from the statement: 'This month's quota depends on last month's surplus'. Quotas are more important in times of mortgage famine, when money is **tight**. When it is **easy**, and **mortgage funds** are in ready supply, they become insignificant.

2 In life assurance, as in building societies, a limited sum of money. However, whereas in building societies the sum has a movable upper limit, in life assurance the limit is a lower one. A branch manager may be told, 'Your quota for life figures for next year will be *x* hundred thousand pounds'.

Quota well illustrates the entangled ramifications of financial usage. In the one profession, a *quota* is a figure not to be exceeded; in the other, a figure which must be at least achieved.

R

reassign
See **assign**

records clerk
See **control**

refer
In banking, to ensure that **funds** are available in an account, or if not, to obtain managerial authority, before cashing a cheque.

See also **black list**

reference list
See **black list**

refer to drawer
In banking, an **answer** written on a cheque returned unpaid for lack of **funds**, advising the beneficiary to contact the signatory to the cheque.

refer to drawer, please represent
In banking, as in the preceding entry, but suggesting also that if the cheque is **presented** again there is the possibility that it will be paid. Second and (if need be) subsequent presentations are normally effected on behalf of customers by the bank simply putting the offending cheques back into the **clearing** system.

regularize
See **correct**

regulated products
Those services (see **product**) which are sold by banks and building societies but which are outside their mainstream

accounts. Life **assurance** policies and pensions would fall into this category, and are regulated in the sense that, when selling them, the institutions are guided by the **Securities and Investment Board** or one of the **self-regulating organizations**, such as the **Life Assurance and Unit Trust Regulatory Organization**.

remittance

In banking, building societies and life assurance, a sum of money sent from one person to another. When a banker writes to an overdrawn customer, 'I must ask you please to ensure that no further cheques are issued until the present overdrawn balance is repaid and a remittance is credited to the account', the term occurs as one of the financial community's various ways of avoiding saying *money* (see also **funds**, and *effects* under **answer**). Not surprisingly, the section in some banks which deals with putting cheques into the **clearing**, i.e. remitting them to the banks on which they are drawn, is itself known as *remittances*.

remittances

See **batch sheet**

repayment mortgage

In banking and building societies, one of the two most common types of **mortgage**, where the borrower repays both capital and interest during the term of the loan. See also **endowment mortgage** and **term assurance**.

representative

In banking, building societies and life assurance, someone who acts for a particular company. When giving **best advice**, all a representative needs to do is to recommend the best of that particular company's **products** (or to indicate that it has nothing suitable to offer). This puts a representative in marked contrast to an **independent financial adviser**.

reserve

In banking, cash not held on the counter, or which is not required there: 'We'll put the reserve in the safe'. In some banks, it refers to the safe itself: 'Can we go into the reserve, please?'

S

S & I
See **Scotch and Irish**

salesman
See **inspector**

Save As You Earn

In banking and building societies, describing a scheme aimed at regular savers, which offers them guaranteed returns on their money at the end of five years' saving and even more if the accumulated funds are left for another two years. The monthly schemes are available only through banks and building societies. The name is obviously modelled on the rather less popular Pay As You Earn (PAYE) tax system.

say

In banking, building societies and life assurance, a device for signalling that a sum of money already given in figures is, to avoid any possibility of mistake, now to be repeated in words. French correspondents use *Je dis* ('I say') in equivalent contexts. The *Oxford English Dictionary* mentions the English usage in its discussion of *say* as a marker of approximation:

> In commercial documents *say* is also used, without any implication of inexactness, to introduce any varied repetition of a numerical or quantitative statement: eg 'a shipment of 215 (say two hundred and fifteen) tons of coal'.

No citations appear from acknowledged, dated sources, but letters from bankers show the usage to have been established well over 100 years ago.

SAYE
See **Save As You Earn**

Scotch and Irish (S & I)

In banking, applied to banknotes issued by Scottish or Irish banks (see **country notes**); also applied to cheques drawn on branches of banks in Scotland or Ireland. *Scotch and Irish* also refers to the section of a **batch sheet** in which Scotch and Irish cheques are **listed**.

Scotch may strike one as being unusually colloquial to appear in formal surroundings. *Scottish*, which is steadily replacing *Scotch* in literary and educated usage, is the more usual adjective. Thus, a new **remittances** clerk may be told, 'Scottish cheques go in Scotch and Irish.' Indeed, it seems likely that it is its status as part of an established phrase that has allowed *Scotch* to remain unaltered in this context. It is a fossilized term, comparable with elements in *hale and hearty* or *might and main*, where, in the first case, the adjective *hale* is now only very rarely used outside the phrase, and, in the second, the noun *main* is given the sense of 'physical force' only in this particular usage.

secs and recs

In banking, an abbreviation used within at least one bank to refer to its head office's *Securities and Recoveries Department*. Not only is the abbreviation easier to say, but its homophony with *sex and wrecks* enables branch staff to have what appears to be a very thinly disguised joke at the expense of their head office superiors.

securities

In banking, documents of value, such as property deeds, life assurance policies, or share certificates, deposited with a bank as a condition of the granting of a **loan**. The department of a bank handling these carries the same title, which sometimes turns out to be less than helpful to customers for whom a sign marked *Securities* over a section of the counter separated from the **cashiers** conjures up the image of guards responsible for the protection of the premises and its valuable contents. The idea tends to be reinforced by their overhearing other customers asking for **deed boxes** to be brought from the safe, or for some precious items to be placed in *safe custody*.

In fact, the banker's use of the word derives from the fact that it is the repayment of the relevant debt which is *secured* by these documents. Because such items are also frequently left with banks purely for safe keeping, they are normally handled by the same departmental staff—hence the requests referred to above.

Securities and Investment Board (SIB)

The company in the UK which is at the top of the hierarchy of the organizations concerned with safeguarding investors. Under the 1986 Financial Services Act, the Secretary of State for Trade and Industry has delegated powers to this board to assist in the process of regulating the professional dealings of those giving investment advice. The board is itself aided by the **self-regulating organizations** and recognized professional bodies, but it should always be remembered that, in the end, no one can actually stop you from doing the investor's equivalent of backing a three-legged donkey.

self-regulating organizations

Five bodies in the UK set up under the Secretary of State for Trade and Industry to assist the **Securities and Investment Board** in controlling the activities of investment businesses, thereby giving the public some degree of protection. The five are: the **Association of Futures Brokers & Dealers (AFBD)**; the **Financial Intermediaries, Managers & Brokers Regulatory Association (FIMBRA)**; the **Investment Management Regulatory Organization (IMRO)**; the **Life Assurance & Unit Trust Regulatory Organization (LAUTRO)**; and **The Securities Association (TSA)**.

Other professional bodies, such as the various Law Societies and the Institute of Actuaries, carry out similar functions.

service

In banking and building societies, to make interest payments on a **loan**. The word is increasingly in use in banking and building society circles: 'We need to be certain that our customer's income is sufficient to service a loan of this size.' This usage is comparatively recent, and would appear to be an extension of the sense 'maintain' in phrases such as to *service a car*.

set off

In banking, to allow **funds** held on one account to enter into the calculation of **debit** interest charged on money borrowed on another account, with the effect of reducing that interest charge; hence also the noun, *set-off*. Both the verb and the noun are frequently used in conjunction with **turn**. If, for example, a customer has £1000 in a **deposit account** and simultaneously owes £2000 on a **loan** account, the bank may be asked to *set off* the one amount against the other, so that interest is paid on only the net £1000. This would be termed a *full set-off*, and is fairly rare. What the bank would be more likely to agree to would be a *set-off with a turn*. This would result in full interest being charged on the £1000 and a *turn* of (say) two per cent—in other words, an effective interest rate—being charged on the rest.

share account

In building societies, the ordinary type of savings account offered by societies, so called because the holder becomes a member of the society, unlike **deposit account** counterparts.

short cast

See **cast**

short term money

See **hot money**

shot coin

In banking, loose, unbagged coin. The phrase is in use in all the clearing banks. **Cashiers** opening a canvas bag of £100 of silver would expect to find therein 20 separate bags each containing £5—**bagged coin**. Sometimes, however, they have the misfortune to discover that some of these bags have opened or burst, depositing their contents into the bottom of the outer bag. Coin in this state is described as being *shot* (the adjective may be used attributively or predicatively). Although, happily, these occurrences are much less common since polythene bags have superseded paper, the phrase persists. New coin from the Royal Mint always comes loose in, say, £100 bags, and it is from the minting process that the term seems to be derived—coin is *shot* into hoppers on the minting and sorting machines. Although the term hardly ever appears in print, it is ubiquitous amongst bankers and coin-producers in Britain, and its continued use marks the strength of the oral tradition in financial circles.

shotter
See **fly-balance**

SIB
See **Securities and Investment Board**

sighter
See **fly-balance**

sort code, also sorting code, sorting code number
In banking, the six-figure number shown in three pairs at the top right-hand corner of a cheque, and reprinted for electronic reading at the bottom. Each branch of each bank has its unique number, and anyone wishing to receive money from an account, for example by **direct debit** or **standing order**, or to pay money into it, will require this number.

source book
In building societies, a book used to record the provenance of all **funds** other than those paid in over the counter.

See also **brokerage**

split investment
In banking and building societies, as its name suggests, an avoidance of putting all one's financial eggs in one basket. A split investment might involve, for example, so much of a customer's **funds** going into a **deposit account** to which there is effectively immediate access, so much into one where interest rates are higher but notice to withdraw is required, so much into unit trusts, and so on. It is likely to result from **portfolio selling**.

standing order

In banking, a term now used by most customers and staff in preference to the older **banker's order**.

See also **mandate 3** and **direct debit**

statement re mutilation requires banker's confirmation

See **answer**

statistics

In banking, information collected by branches on, for example, the number of transactions on a certain customer's account, and normally abbreviated to **stats**. It can be extended to act as an appellation for the person collecting the information—'Who's stats this week?' This short form of the word is not, of course, peculiar to bankers. Students in educational institutions throughout the land may be heard to complain that 'Maths is OK—it's the stats I find difficult.'

stub

See **counterfoil**

surplus

See **net receipts**

surrender value

In life assurance, the sum offered when you wish to cash in a policy. As indicated under **front end loading**, the expenses associated with life assurance are charged in the early days of a policy. This is the principal reason why, if you find you cannot afford to continue paying the **premiums** and want to cash in your policy, you may well find that the surrender value is less than the total of the premiums paid to that point. Compare **paid up policy** for what is often a preferable alternative to surrender.

survivance

In life assurance, survival. If a letter from a life assurance company accepting a **proposal** carries the words 'On survivance of the Life Assured to the Annuity Date', its meaning is presumably clear enough, but its use lends an element of legal archaism to the language of the letter. The *Oxford English Dictionary* cites from a statute enacted in 1874: 'A personal right . . . shall . . . vest . . . in the heir . . . by his survivance of the person to whom he is entitled to succeed.'

SV

In building societies, the initial letters of **signature verification**, referring to the process of checking the normally invisible signature that many societies now arrange for their customers to provide in their **passbooks**, and which can be read only under ultra-violet light. The abbreviation appears in its most bewildering form to customers when **cashiers** use it as a verb: 'Can we SV your book?'

T

take a charge
See **charge**

take-out
The informal name in one building society for the form on which **cashiers** enter figures to **balance** at the end of the business day. Its rarely used 'proper' title is *Transaction List and Balancing Summary*. Small wonder, therefore, that a shorter substitute title has been found.

See also **till reconciliation**

Tax Exempt Special Savings Account
In banking and building societies, an account which offers the attraction of tax-free saving within carefully prescribed limits. It was featured in the UK in the 'saver's budget' of 1990, became available in January 1991, and has generally been given the acronym **TESSA**. Only one TESSA is allowed per adult; regular savings must not exceed £150 per month; and a total investment is restricted to £9000 over the normal five-year life of the account.

technical irregularities
In banking, errors in a cheque made in writing it out. A common error is the use of the previous year's date during the first few days of January. Technical irregularities, as reasons for returning a cheque unpaid, contrast with the possibility of its return for lack of **funds**.

See also **answer, in order** and **present (for payment)** for further discussion.

Tees
In banking, the common abbreviation for *Trustees* in account titles.

See also **ors**

telegraphic transfer

In banking, a method of transferring sums of money abroad, between banks, by telegraphic means; usually abbreviated to **TT**, and also now more often known as a *priority payment*.

teller

In banking and building societies, a **cashier**. Although the *Oxford English Dictionary* has various citations going as far back as 1480 for *teller* in this sense, it is rarely used in the UK (at least by staff, and probably not much more so by customers). The spread of **automated teller machines** might have led to an increase in the currency of *teller*, had they not been reduced in speech to *ATMs* by the institutions and *cash dispensers* by the public.

tens

In banking and building societies in the UK, 10 pence pieces or £10 notes; in the USA, $10 bills.

See Appendix 2 for a discussion of the functions of financial terminology.

term assurance

An inexpensive form of life **assurance**, because it pays out only if the assured person dies within a specified time. Once the term has expired, there is nothing due to the holder. It is quite popular with those who perceive the need for a high level of cover but not for the whole of their (working) lives. Thus, one group of people to whom it is attractive are parents who wish to secure the financial well-being of their offspring, but only until the latter become self-sufficient. In a different but related scenario, businesses can choose to protect themselves for a specified period of time against the untimely loss of a pivotal partner or employee—see **keyman assurance**.

Decreasing term policies are commonly taken out by mortgagors who have traditional **repayment mortgages**. As the loan is repaid, so the cover reduces, with both eventually (and simultaneously) arriving at nil. As the intention is to allow the loan to be repaid if the borrower dies before the end of the term, these policies are still often known by the older name of *mortgage protection policies*.

terminal operator

In banking and building societies, a person operating the device which links a branch with a central or regional computer (see **node point**) and often still called a **machinist**.

TESSA

See **Tax Exempt Special Savings Account**

The Securities Association (TSA)

One of the five **self-regulating organizations** in the UK assisting the **Securities and Investment Board** in providing some measure of protection to investors, as authorized by the Secretary of State for Trade and Industry under the Financial Services Act of 1986.

ticker

In banking, the assistant to an **inspector**. The primary function of a ticker is to certify the accuracy of entries in a branch's accounts and other records. The term is normally restricted to talking about, rather than to, the person concerned:

Is John Smith an inspector now? No, he's only a ticker.

As with *doggy*, a term used by colliery faceworkers for a deputy, who 'dogs' or follows the men around, there is a degree of ambivalence in the apparent denigration involved. On the one hand, the term suggests a certain contempt for one who is only an assistant, 'not the real thing'—compare *doggy* with *monkey* in 'I want to talk to the organ-grinder not the monkey.' On the other hand, there is no doubt that many of the underlings—faceworkers and bank clerks alike—envy the butts of these appellations their superior positions and pay.

tight

In building societies, applied to **mortgage funds** in short supply. The term is also applied generally to situations where money supply is restricted.

See **easy**

till

In banking and building societies, the drawers and cupboards in which **cashiers** keep cash during the day. Bankers extend *till* to cover the contents as well as the container—that is, the money kept in the till is itself known as *the till*. If a cashier fails to balance at the end of the day and cannot find any errors in the entries or additions in the record kept of cash transactions, a colleague is sure to remark, 'It must be in your till.' This does not mean that the colleague thinks that the discrepancy (see **difference**) is to be accounted for by money overlooked in the till drawers. Instead, it is the banker's shorthand for 'It [the difference between the **debit** and the **credit** totals] must be a result of your having miscounted the cash left at the close of business [the till].' This same till is used to commence business the following day.

For an analogous transference of title from container to contents, compare **pipeline** in building-society usage.

till reccy

See **till reconciliation**

till reconciliation

In building societies, a form on which **cashiers** in one society enter figures to balance at the end of the business day. It is the equivalent of the *Transaction List and Balancing Summary* in another society, and just as that particular mouthful is avoided by the substitute term **take-out**, so a till reconciliation is, to the staff concerned, never anything more than a *till reccy*.

time out

In banking and building societies, used of a plastic card that has been retained in the **bin** of an **automated teller machine** because the customer has not taken the card back before the time allowed has expired. On entering the branch to retrieve the card, the customer may be offered the explanation, 'The machine ate your card because it timed out.' The phrase derives from the everyday expression 'to run out of time', and has no connection with the American games term meaning a break in play.

T of E
See **transfer of equity**

town
See **country**

transaction list and balancing summary
See **take-out**

transfer of equity (T of E)
In banking and building societies, a term borrowed from law and applied to a situation where there is some change in the name of a mortgagor—for example, on the marriage, divorce or death of one or more of the holders of a **mortgage** account held in joint names. It is somewhat misleading in the financial context. Although there may be some **equity** (the property's net value to the customer), the institution is more concerned with transferring the exact opposite—that is, the debt owed to it and secured against the property.

trigger list
See **black list**

truncation
In banking, the electronic transfer of **funds** within the United Kingdom, eliminating the physical conveyance of paper **vouchers**. The time taken is usually shorter too.

TSA
See **The Securities Association**

turn
1 In banking, relating to foreign currency, the difference between the buying and selling rates quoted by a bank. If, for example, the rates for the French franc are (buying) £1 = FF9.90 and (selling) £1 = FF9.40, a **foreign clerk** may remark to colleagues, 'I see we're taking a fifty centime turn on the French franc'.

See also **buy high, sell low**

2 Also in banking, relating to interest rates, the excess of a rate charged over a bank's **base rate**. Not all customers enjoy the same standing with their bank manager, who can exercise discretion in deciding the rate to be charged for lending money—generally speaking, the higher the risk, the higher the rate. Lending rates are calculated against a published base rate. If a bank's base rate is 17 per cent, and a customer is to be charged 20 per cent, the manager can record that the branch is 'taking a turn of three over base rate'. This turn is also occasionally referred to as the *added rate*, for obvious reasons.

See also **set off**

Both these usages (currency and interest rates) are themselves borrowed from another institution: dealers on the Stock Exchange make their profit from what is called the *turn of the market*. The *Oxford English Dictionary* cites the following definition from the *Counting House Dictionary* of 1882: 'the difference between the two prices quoted in the official lists for stocks, shares, etc'. The use of *turn* by clerks thus not only confirms their status as bankers, but also announces their membership of the wider financial community.

twenties

In banking and building societies in the UK, 20 pence coins and £20 notes; in the USA, $20 bills.

See Appendix 2 for a discussion of the functions of financial terminology.

twos

In banking and building societies in the UK, two pence coins.

See Appendix 2 for a discussion of the functions of financial terminology.

226A cover

In life assurance, a former pension plan for the self-employed or those not in a scheme provided by their employers. It took its name from the section of the Finance Act that permitted such schemes, and was replaced by personal pensions in the Social Security Act in July 1988.

U

underwrite
See **write**

unit trust
In banking, building societies and life assurance, an organization (of which there are many) which allows individuals, effectively, to invest in a large number of companies—something that would otherwise be possible for only the wealthy minority. It does this by selling units to the public and then using the collected **funds** to buy shares or make such other investments as are permitted. The units are then representations of the elements of the trust's total funds held by particular investors.

up
In banking, building societies and life assurance, applied to a situation where one is able to obtain information from a computer terminal: 'the terminal', 'the branch' or simply 'we' can all be said to be *up*. Its opposite is *down*.

See also *lock out*

V

voucher
In banking, building societies and life assurance, any piece of paper supporting a bookkeeping entry, such as a paying-in slip, cheque, or internal document.

W

walks

In banking, the section of a **batch sheet** which lists cheques drawn on London institutions that are not members of the **clearing house** (see also **Scotch and Irish**). Payment of cheques drawn on such banks is obtained by clerks or messengers of the **collecting banks** who **present** the cheques at the drawee banks. This explains why those messengers work in the **Walks** departments of their banks, and why a new **remittances** clerk in a branch, wondering what to do with a cheque drawn on an unfamiliar bank, will be told, 'Put it in Walks': the final stage of its clearing will involve, quite simply, someone walking with the cheque to the drawee bank.

waste

In banking, paying-in slips, cheques, etc paid into a branch during a working day, or the process for handling them. As indicated under **batch**, when these items have been passed behind the counter, they are listed on temporary sheets to ensure that they **balance** against each other. These sheets are known in some banks as *waste sheets*—*waste* in the sense that they may be destroyed after the transactions have been permanently recorded on customers' accounts. The *Oxford English Dictionary* defines *waste-book* in the following way:

a rough account-book (now little used in ordinary business) in which entries are made of all transactions . . . at the time of their occurrence, to be 'posted' afterwards in the more formal books of the set.

Waste sheets are clearly the banks' equivalents of such books. However, the originally adjectival *waste* in the phrase has subsequently been freed to act as a noun, indicating either the items at the time of initial processing, or the process itself: 'I think we've got enough now to put through the waste.'

It is easy to understand the logic of this, even if it is mistaken. If a *cash book* is a book in which one lists cash, then a *waste sheet* must be a sheet on which one lists waste. There is a nicely comparable process to be observed in the formation of the twentieth century slang term for a cigarette—*fag*—from *fag-end*, which has been in use from at least the early seventeenth century to mean a remnant of any kind. The *Oxford English Dictionary* records, amongst various examples, 'There's the fag-end of a leg of mutton' (1613) and 'The fag-end of this last century' (1656).

This initial checking via waste sheets is fast disappearing from branch work. The term is, of course, going with it.

white book
See **colour terms**

with/without profits
See **assurance**

write
In life assurance, to effect **assurance** cover. The well-known term *underwriting* derives quite simply from the practice of members of syndicates signing their names under the risk (or part of the risk) that they will cover, particularly in marine insurance at Lloyd's. Probably less well known is the construction involving *write* in life assurance **offices**. In order to outlaw the use of life policies as instruments of gambling, the Life Assurance Act of 1774 introduced the notion of 'insurable interest'. Briefly, this means that X, to be able to effect assurance on the life of Y, must be able to demonstrate that he or she would suffer financial loss as a result of Y's death. A husband and wife clearly have this insurable interest in each other. Perhaps less obviously, a manufacturing company which depended substantially on the personal charisma of its sales manager could demonstrate a similar interest. 'Buying in' a replacement member of staff from another company, or training someone from within the organization, would involve, respectively, an increase in expenditure or a drop in revenue.

Wherever this insurable interest exists and a policy is taken out, the assured will normally think of the assurance company as the active party in the provision of the policy. Grammatical structures in conversation between members of life assurance staff, however, would suggest the opposite. Commonplace are comments such as 'a wife may write a policy on the life of her husband' and 'commercial or industrial employers can write policies on their key staff'.

See also **keyman assurance**

The *Oxford English Dictionary* gives *write* as a synonym for *underwrite*, but the examples cited illustrate the verb being used only where the grammatical subject is the insurer, not the client—for example, 'Not all insurance companies have felt justified in writing the risks' (*The Times*, 1931).

APPENDIX I

Etymological Notes

If we consider the origins of certain words discussed in the previous pages, an etymological pattern emerges. *Advise, agent, assurance, bill, collection, credit, current, debit, deposit, draft, equity, favour, funds, honour, life, loan, mature, mortgage, policy, premium* and *remittance* are, especially when two or three are gathered together, powerful indicators of banking/building society/life assurance English. Of these words, only *draft* (with its related forms *draw, overdraw,* etc), *life* and *loan* are of Germanic origin; all the others share a Latin ancestry. Furthermore, only *agent, deposit, funds* and *premium* have been taken directly from Latin, the majority having come into Middle English via Old French. One does not have to search far for the reasons: for long after the conquest, all posts of any importance were filled by Normans, whose language naturally entered into their work. The great financial institutions had their birth some centuries later, but it was inevitable, given the underlying legal framework, that the members of these institutions should turn to the law, with its language strongly influenced by Old French, as a source of their own particular terms.

The words discussed above are those which, although indicative of the 'finance variety', are all freely used in correspondence with customers. If we now consider those that are usually restricted to behind-the-counter conversation, an interesting change in the pattern of derivations occurs. Here, only a few words are of Romance origin—*indent, portfolio, quota*. The majority comprises words with Germanic roots—*float, house, pipeline, shot, shotter, walks*. Additionally, there are the hybrid formations *fly balance* and *hot money*, where Germanic modifiers have been placed before Romance nouns. It comes as no surprise to discover that, in their efforts both to enliven a language so heavily laden with a polysyllabic Latinate vocabulary, and to promote social cohesion among their colleagues, financial staff have injected strong doses of words that were in everyday use half a millenium before the Norman conquest. A final comment from one building society manager is superbly apposite: when asked if he used any special term to describe something that balanced exactly at the first attempt, he replied, 'No—just the usual Anglo-Saxon expletives when it doesn't.'

APPENDIX II

Functions of In-house Language

There is a remarkable absence, especially amongst bank and building society cashiers, of slang terms for money. This is at first surprising, given that (a) in everyday use there are many such items of usage (*note, bar, sheet, fiver, tenner*, and the newer ones such as *Jack* and *Placido* being only a few examples) and (b) one's experience of bank and building-society clerks does not lead one to believe that they are of significantly more serious disposition than other people of their age and education. An explanation may be found in the field of social control.

Terms
In the research study which formed the foundation of the present book, the following terms were found to be in common use by all personnel interviewed and/or observed:

Denomination	Common Name (in plural)
Coins	
1p and £1	Ones
2p	Twos
5p	Fives
10p	Tens
20p	Twenties
50p	Fifties
Notes	
£5	Fives
£10	Tens
£20	Twenties
£50	Fifties

Appendix II

In British society, there would seem to be three distinguishable levels of usage where cash is concerned. The most formal is to be found in restricted circumstances, notably in the context of government publications and serious news announcements: 'Following the introduction of the smaller five pence piece . . .'; 'The new five pound note bears the likeness of the inventor George Stephenson.' The least formal is probably used by everybody (including financial staff when not in their professional personae) in colloquial conversation: 'Can you lend me a fiver?'; 'Here's a couple of tenners.' The intermediate level, of particular interest here, is associated, though not exclusively, with the staffs of financial institutions. The delimiting condition appears to be that the user of this level is actively engaged in handling money belonging to someone else as part of his or her daily work, so that the comments to be made below may have equal validity in relation to, for instance, a cashier in a supermarket.

The basis of the nomenclature is obvious enough: the cashiers refer to all denominations of notes and coins simply by the units involved. Observe that this applies even though the risk of ambiguity is potentially high: *fives, tens, twenties* and *fifties* are all used for both notes and coins, where the former are worth one hundred times more than the latter. Why should this be?

First, one must remark on the level of formality. The terms used are not the 'official' ones (eg *five pound notes*), but, given the wide range of slang terms available in the language, they are strikingly formal and serious—and it is this very seriousness that provides a partial explanation for their use. Handling large amounts of other people's money is a serious affair, and the language used reflects that situation. Whether it is merely a reflection is something we shall return to shortly.

To reach the complement of this explanation we must first focus on what is omitted: the words *pence* and *pounds*. It is easy to see these as indicators of particular denominations of money, but what may be overlooked is that they also indicate money itself. There are good reasons for using linguistic forms here which direct the handlers' attention away from the precise nature of what they are handling. Customers who may never see more than a few hundred pounds in cash at any one time are naturally curious to know the effect on cashiers of handling hundreds of thousands. The question was constantly asked during the author's own time as a bank cashier, and the practice continues unabated today. Now, only the most iron-willed people could resist temptation if they were constantly looking in their tills and saying to themselves, 'I've got fifty thousand pounds there.' As a protective measure, therefore, the cashier habitually refers to and thinks of the cash as, for example, 'ten thousand in twenties, twenty thousand in tens, and twenty thousand in fives'.

Notice the power of this defence mechanism: it protects the cashier from crime and the institution from loss. It is not surprising, therefore, that the defence is dropped only in cases of absolute necessity, ie to disambiguate requests:

Cashier A: Have you got twenty pounds in fives?

Cashier B offers four bags, each containing five pounds of five pence pieces.

Cashier A: No, I meant £5 notes.

These seemingly very simple devices, then, manage to serve, simultaneously, two ostensibly conflicting ends—to discourage a flippant attitude towards money, and yet to avoid concentrating the cashier's attention on the desirability of the stock-in-trade. There is a nice irony in the fact that professions which pride themselves on their integrity actually promote, through language, a kind of occupational schizophrenia in their employees.

APPENDIX III

A Case Study

Whilst many of the entries in the main body of this work show items used in context, they share the problem, encountered in all dictionaries, of being discussed in isolation from one another. The following small-scale case study may be found helpful as a way of remedying that situation; it will also give us the opportunity to consider some matters of grammar, which are normally largely outside the realm of the lexicographer.

To avoid the possibility of identification of those involved in the production of the original letters, only extracts are employed. The letters in question are part of a series designed to be sent to those disreputable characters who insist on trying to run up unauthorized overdrafts.

The first letter, having informed the customer of the state of indebtedness, takes the gentlest possible line, with the sentence *We are advising you so that any error on our part or yours may be corrected.* By simply *advising* that the account is overdrawn, and by the use of *error* and *corrected*, not only does the letter avoid laying the blame directly at the customer's door; sincerely or otherwise, it suggests that the situation may have been created unintentionally. The impersonal structures (*is overdrawn, may be corrected*) are, of course, vital here, but the syntax of the second sentence is especially noteworthy. The usual 'courtesy' position for a pronoun which relates to the writer and which is coordinated with other nouns or pronouns is at the very end of the construction—*John and I, neither yours nor mine.* In the present case, however, to remove the accusation of responsibility for even an accidental misdemeanour as far as possible away from the customer, the syntax is inverted to produce *any error on our part or yours.*

The second letter is for a customer whose account occasionally fluctuates into debit. Many of the lexical items employed show a heavy dependence on clichés. These are not necessarily 'commercialese'; they may simply be the ready-made phrases that are available for use by anyone in a position of authority who finds it necessary to issue a mild rebuke. For example, the opening reference to the varying fortunes of the account—*I am surprised to find*—has a distinctly headmasterly ring to it, while *I wish to take this opportunity to remind you* (in this case about the conditions under which certain other facilities are granted) is possible within many formal contexts.

The letter ends with the following paragraph:

> It may be that you are meeting some exceptional costs at this time and if this is the case I shall be pleased to discuss the problem with you. Meanwhile I shall be pleased if you will advise me when funds will be available to repay the present overdraft.

The repetition of *I shall be pleased* comes as no surprise, given the fondness for its use by business letter writers in general. Nor does its use, on the second occasion, with *if you will advise me*. As indicated under the entry for *advise*, that word, in the sense of 'inform', is still much favoured by writers in financial institutions. So, too, is *funds*. When lenders use a phrase such as *mortgage funds*, the sense is of money earmarked for that particular purpose; in the present letter, it seems to have the more general sense of money in all its manifestations. (Readers may wish to consult relevant entries for a discussion of the possible reasons for the avoidance of such an 'ordinary' word as *money* in these contexts.)

Grammatically, the letter follows the pattern of its precursor by using constructions that avoid the mention of individuals in unpleasant circumstances. Accounts are seemingly responsible for their own conduct (*account is becoming overdrawn, Current Account should remain in credit*); certainly no one is explicitly blamed for the undesirable state of affairs. Where less distressing matters are concerned (*I wish to take this opportunity, I shall be pleased*), or where the wording suggests some sympathy with the reader's predicament (*you are meeting some exceptional costs*), then the writer uses the active voice.

Next in the series is a letter that would be sent to a customer who, far from acceding to the bank's request to put affairs in order, actually increases the indebtedness. After reminding the customer (by means of *May I please refer*) of the earlier letters which pointed to *the balance of the account* being *overdrawn without agreement*, the writer says:

> Since that time further cheques have been presented with the result that the overdrawn balance is now increased to £x. In the circumstances, I must ask you please to ensure that no further cheques are issued until the present overdrawn balance is repaid and a remittance credited to the account to enable any other cheques already issued but not presented for payment to be met when they are received by the Bank.

The preceding letter dealt with matters which, whilst not desirable, were not of great moment to the bank, and many of the phrases used were open to officials working in other fields. Here, however, things are much more serious: unauthorized over-drafts and the possibility of having to return cheques for lack of funds are the stuff of which writers of textbooks on the practice of banking thrive. Not surprisingly, therefore, this letter shows a swift retreat into the specialized terminology of banking. In addition to *balance of your account, overdrawn without arrangement* and *overdrawn balance*, we find *presented* (and *presented for payment*), *issued, remittance, credited* and *met*.

Once again, the grammatical structures employed are all such as to minimize personal involvement, and, with it, acrimony. One may note especially the way in which the writer excuses the requests by ostensibly shifting the onus: *May I please refer* apparently (if not actually) requests the reader's permission for the writer to make the point, while *I must ask you* suggests compulsion from an authority higher than the writer. Elsewhere, the financier's old friend the impersonal passive holds dominion: *cheques have been presented, balance is now increased, no further cheques are issued, balance is repaid, remittance is credited*.

Whilst the repeated use of the word *please* helps to establish an atmosphere of politeness, it is its syntactic positioning, together with the related graphological matter of punctuation, that is more interesting. Had the letter begun *May I refer you, please, to ..., please*, enclosed in parenthetic commas, would have appeared as a mere courtesy word. Its deliberate placing before the main verb and without commas increases the note of insistency. It is only one step removed from emphasizing the word by graphological variation, such as by underscoring or the use of upper-case type. Similarly, *I must ask you please to ensure* is at once both more formal and more pressing than *to please ensure* or *to ensure, please*, would have been. There is also, of course, the strong possibility that a prescriptive grammar is at least partly responsible for the avoidance of a split infinitive.

If all else has failed, the customer receives the final demand:

> Despite my previous letters advising you that your account is overdrawn ... I appear to have had no reply and the balance remains the same. If I do not receive from you a remittance within the course of the next seven days, I regret I shall have no alternative but to seek recovery by employing the legal remedies available to the Bank.

Although the 'pleases' may have disappeared, efforts are still made to maintain an air of courtesy (*I regret*) and even at this stage to allow for the possibility of some factor outside the control of the protagonists—*I appear to have had no reply.* *Advising, account, overdrawn, balance* and *remittance* all occur as they did in earlier letters. *Within the course of the next seven days* and *I regret I shall have no alternative but to . . .* are both part of the formula used by writers in many circumstances as the preamble to a threat to enforce payment of a debt through the courts. The words following the preamble in this particular case are interesting in so far as they diverge from the more usual *place the matter in the hands of our solicitors*. Here, the banker puts fewer restrictions on the options: *the legal remedies available to the Bank* could also include, for instance, using the services of a debt-collecting agency.

As indicated above, an air of cold politeness pervades the letter. However, whereas up to this point we have repeatedly had occasion to remark on the use of the passive voice to maintain social distance and avoid unpleasantness, now there is a quite dramatic shift into the active: *If I do not now receive, I regret, I shall.* The niceties of the impersonal construction have disappeared; however distasteful it may be, the time has come for direct, no-nonsense communication.

With that point in mind, it is worth, finally, reflecting here on the guidance given in a house style manual to writers, urging the active voice in preference to the passive. One cannot help wondering whether the instruction, which manages so neatly to exemplify exactly the construction that it sets out to condemn—rather like saying that 'a preposition is a word that you shouldn't end a sentence with'—was written tongue in cheek, or whether a sort of financial Imp of the Perverse was at work: *The passive form, with its impersonal aloofness, is not recommended.*